WEANING
and First Foods

NICOLA GRAIMES

hamlyn

An Hachette UK company
www.hachette.co.uk

First published in Great Britain in 2009 by
Carroll & Brown Publishers Limited

This second edition published in 2015 by Hamlyn,
a division of Octopus Publishing Group Ltd
Carmelite House
50 Victoria Embankment
London
EC4Y 0D7
www.octopusbooks.co.uk

Copyright © Octopus Publishing Group Ltd 2009, 2015

ISBN 978-0-600-63145-3

A CIP catalogue record for this book is available from the
British Library.

Printed and bound in China

10 9 8 7 6 5 4 3 2 1

All reasonable care has been taken in the preparation of this
book but the information it contains is not intended to take
the place of treatment by a qualified medical practitioner.

The Department of Health advises that eggs should not be
consumed raw. This book contains dishes made with raw or
lightly cooked eggs. It is prudent for babies and young
children to avoid uncooked or lightly cooked dishes made
with eggs. Once prepared these dishes should be kept
refrigerated and used promptly.
This book includes dishes made with nuts and nut
derivatives. It is advisable for customers with known allergic
reactions to nuts and nut derivatives and those who may be
potentially vulnerable to these allergies, such as babies and
children, to avoid dishes made with nuts and nut oils. It is
also prudent to check the labels of pre-prepared ingredients
for the possible inclusion of nut derivatives.

CONTENTS

Preface 4

WEANING

When to start 6

Stage 1: Introducing solids 7

Stage 2: Increasing the menu 14

Stage 3: Three meals a day 18

Stage 4: Family meals 24

From one year 26

From two years 33

RECIPES

First foods 42

Breakfast 56

Snacks & sides 68

Light meals 84

Main meals 94

Puddings & bakes 128

Index 142

Acknowledgements 144

Many parents feel slightly daunted by the prospect of weaning their baby and I can recall feeling exactly the same with my daughter. I had got to grips with breastfeeding but the next stage of actually introducing solid food to her diet seemed a bit scary – a journey into the unknown. The combination of a desire to do the best for her and the various bits of advice from well-meaning friends and family conspired to add to my uncertainty. My nerves proved unnecessary as weaning didn't prove as difficult as I had predicted but I know my concerns were not out of the ordinary.

My aim in writing this book is to ease any concerns other parents may have and to give a practical and reassuring guide to feeding babies and toddlers. Welcome weaning as an exciting stage in your baby's life and a natural part of her development. Bear in mind that the principle of weaning (the process of replacing a baby's total dependence on milk with "solid" foods) is to gradually introduce her to a wide range of tastes and textures until she can eventually enjoy the same meals as the rest of the family. The emphasis is on gradual, so take it slowly and enjoy this new stage in your baby's development.

Be prepared for mess and enjoy the ride!

PREFACE

When to Start Weaning

Your baby should be ready to start solids at around six months. Until then breast or formula milk meets all of your baby's dietary needs. There are no nutritional advantages to weaning before this age. And, as your baby's immune system is not yet fully developed, there are good reasons not to start before the age of six months.

The British Nutrition Foundation recommends that the majority of babies should start a mixed diet from the age of six months (26 weeks) by which time breast milk and formula do not meet all of their dietary needs. Before four months (17 weeks) a baby's digestive system, notably the gut and kidneys, is too immature to cope with anything more than breast milk or formula. It has been said that weaning too early may make a baby fat and increase the likelihood of allergies; holding off until your baby is six months old can reduce this risk, especially if there is a family history of weight problems and allergies.

However, the guidelines do not fully take into account the wide individual variations in developmental maturity (and appetite) between infants and some are ready for solids slightly before they are six months old – talk to your health visitor if you are unsure. There are three key signs that indicate that your baby is physically ready to start solids: she can stay supported in a sitting position and hold her head steady; she can cooordinate her eyes and hands and pick food up and put it in her mouth by herself; and she can swallow. Signs that can be mistaken for a baby needing solid food such as waking in the night after sleeping through, suddenly needing an extra milk feed, or chewing her fists, are normal behaviour patterns for her age and don't necessarily mean that she is physically ready for solids.

Don't leave weaning much later than six months, unless recommended by your health visitor, because after six months, she needs more nutrients than breast or formula milk provides, particularly of iron. Requirements for protein, thiamine, niacin, vitamins B6 and B12, magnesium, zinc, sodium and chloride also increase between the ages of six and 12 months. She will only get these nutrients if she begins to have a varied diet with food from all the main food groups.

Babies who are born pre-term need to be weaned according to their own individual needs and your health visitor or dietician will be able to advise on the best time for your baby.

TO RECAP

- Weaning should be started when your baby is six months (24 weeks) old.
- From the age of six months your baby's nutrient requirements increase, so she needs a diet that includes all the main food groups.
- If think your baby is ready for solid foods earlier, discuss it with your health vistor or doctor first.
- There are foods that must always be avoided before the age of six months.

STAGE 1: Introducing Solids

Weaning is all about getting your baby used to moving food around her mouth that is not liquid. While most foods are suitable for your baby from six months (see page 9 for the exceptions), it's advisable to start gradually, especially if there is a family history of allergies or food intolerance. The first step is to simply familiarise your baby with taking food from a spoon; the food should be smooth, semi-liquid in consistency, with a bland flavour. Initially, the quantity eaten is largely immaterial. If your baby is allowed to self feed, spoon feeding may develop later. Try sitting your baby at the table when you are eating so she gets used to the idea. She may want to try some of your food, too.

Choose a time of day when you are not feeling too rushed or your baby too tired to introduce solids; mid-day is often best. Bear in mind that eating is a new skill for your baby and don't expect her to get it right from the start. She is using previously unused muscles, so don't be put off if food appears to be "spat" out at first – this is perfectly normal. Face-to-face interaction is important: talk to your baby while you feed her; encourage and praise her.

Start gradually – offer some puréed fruit or vegetables (see page 8) on the tip of a plastic spoon or a clean finger. It may be a good idea to give your baby a little milk first to curb any hunger pangs, but as feeding becomes more established, start to offer food before milk. Don't expect your baby to eat more than 1-2 teaspoons at first – although she could well eat more. The first solids should be regarded as a supplement to your baby's milk feed, and you will find that her appetite will vary from one feed to another, so watching how much she is eating every day is not important at this stage. When she loses interest in the food, continue with milk.

For the first few weeks, offer the same food for around three days at a time to allow your baby to get used to new tastes. It is a good idea to keep a food diary to monitor likes and dislikes and gauge if there is any sign of an intolerance or allergy. Signs that your baby may have an allergy include a rash, diarrhoea, bloated tummy or increased gas (see also page 17). Don't be surprised when your baby's stools

did you know…

Until around six months of age, babies have a protective mechanism whereby the tongue pushes forwards, but this then changes and babies begin to be able to take food to the back of the mouth. This explains why in the early stages of weaning it appears that food is being "spat out" or pushed out with the tongue.

? Is your baby ready

All babies are different and progress at their own pace but the following signs may indicate that your baby is ready for weaning. Your baby:

✓ Can sit supported in a sitting position – in a high chair, for example.
✓ Shows an interest in your food.
✓ Makes chewing motions.
✓ Can close her mouth around a spoon.
✓ Holds her head up well.
✓ Can sit up with support.
✓ Can move her tongue back and forth, so she can swallow.
✓ Is teething.

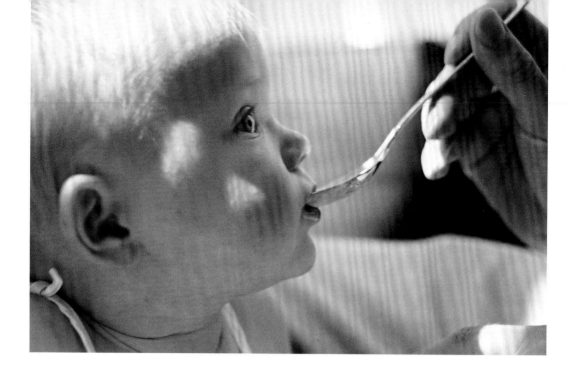

change colour and odour after starting solids. This is perfectly normal. Constipation also is not unusual at this stage. Infant rice cereal, for example, lacks fibre or constipation may be due to dehydration or simply that the digestive

Face-to-face interaction is important: talk to your baby through the feed, trying to be both encouraging and positive.

system is getting used to food. If your baby is constipated, try fruit and vegetables instead of rice as they are richer in fibre, and offer cooled, boiled tap water in a beaker (see page 11).

VERY FIRST FOODS

Start with mild-tasting, single-ingredient purées, for example carrot, parsnip, apple, pear or bananas. Wash or scrub them thoroughly, peel them and remove any core, seeds or pips before cooking. Or you could try dry infant cereal, home-cooked puréed white rice or dry baby rice mixed with breast or formula milk. You can also add vegetables or fruit to the rice. At the early stage, foods should ideally be puréed to a semi-liquid state – the texture of double cream (see page 15).

There is a selection of first food recipes on pages 42 to 45, followed by others suitable once weaning is becoming established. Bear in mind that the age recommendations given are a general guide; please only give foods to your baby when you think she is ready to eat them.

did you know…

Research from the Monell Chemical Senses Center in Philadelphia suggests that young babies are more likely to be successfully weaned on foods to which they have been previously exposed in the womb, or through the traces that make it into breast milk – and that includes broccoli and cabbage. These vegetables have naturally bitter flavours, which children often dislike, but babies may be more open to their tastes if they are already familiar with them.

Babies also are said to be particularly open to new tastes and textures between six to nine months. It has been suggested that parents try providing ingredients individually so infants can taste each one, rather than mixing them together into a single mass.

FOODS TO AVOID

There are a number of seasonings and foodstuffs that should not be given to babies and toddlers (see page 20 for a more in-depth explanation).

Never give the following babies to under six months:

- Salt or hot spices
- Wheat and other grains containing gluten such as barley and rye
- Eggs
- Unpasteurised cheese
- Meat, including liver, and poultry
- Honey and sugar
- Fish and shellfish
- Citrus fruit and juices
- Berries
- Nuts (including peanuts or peanut products) and seeds
- Follow-on formula milk and cow's, goat's and sheep's milk

Never give the following to babies aged six months to one year:

- Salt or hot spices
- Unpasteurised cheese
- Raw or soft cooked eggs
- Honey and sugar
- Shellfish such as prawns and mussels
- Shark, swordfish and marlin (these fish contain relatively high levels of mercury)
- Whole nuts – or any food containing nuts if there is a family history of food allergies
- Cow's, sheep's and goat's milk as a drink

MILK MATTERS

For the first year, breast or formula milk remains a vital source of nutrients for your baby but you may find that as she eats more solid foods, she naturally takes less milk. Yet, if she drinks too much milk then her appetite for solids could be affected and she may begin to lack sufficient nutrients in her diet. In the early stages of weaning, your baby should be still be having at least four bottles of formula or the equivalent

KEEPING THINGS SAFE

Remember to wash your hands with soap before preparing meals and make sure the rest of the family does the same.

Be meticulous with hygiene and cleanliness and make sure all bowls and spoons are sterilised (or washed in the dishwasher) until weaning is established.

Avoid keeping any leftover food for future use or reheating food because it could be a breeding ground for bacteria. Any leftover food should be thrown away.

Never leave your baby alone with food.

Give your baby her own baby-friendly utensils and always stay nearby when she is self-feeding. Go on a first aid course so you can help her if she chokes.

Always check the temperature of your baby's food before your offer it to her. Be especially careful if you heat food in a microwave as it can create hot spots.

If serving food from a jar, ensure that the seal is intact by listening for the popping sound when you open a jar. If the seal has been broken, the food must be thrown away. Spoon out a serving into a separate bowl and keep any remainder stored in the fridge for a maximum of 24 hours. If you buy ready-prepared foods, these should be eaten by their use-by date.

Until she has enough teeth to chew, never give your baby grapes, raisins, cherry tomatoes, popcorn, olives, lumps of meat, cheese, or large pieces of raw vegetables.

GETTING EQUIPPED

There is no need to invest in large amounts of equipment but the following are worth considering:

Bibs – you'll need plenty! There are plenty of types to choose from but the plastic-backed bibs prevent food and drinks soaking through to clothes. The moulded plastic bibs with a trough are more suitable for slightly older babies who have started to feed themselves

2–3 shallow plastic feeding spoons

2 non-slip plastic bowls

Sieve or food mincer

Steamer – while not essential, steaming helps to retain water-soluble nutrients in fruit and vegetables

Feeder cup or beaker with two handles

Mini food processor, hand-held blender and/or liquidiser – again not essential but these make light work of puréeing and finely chopping meals

number of breast-feeds a day. Cow's (also sheep's and goat's) milk can be included in cooking from six months of age but they are not recommended as a main drink until your baby is one year old because they contain too much salt and protein and insufficient iron and other nutrients.

A breastfed baby will take what she needs from the breast; it is not advisable to reduce breastfeeds, as there is no evidence that this will hinder her development. Only give your baby soya-based formula milk if prescribed by your GP or health visitor. Continue to sterilize feeding bottles, as warm milk is a breeding ground for bacteria.

WATER
Before six months of age, fully breast-fed babies should not require additional fluids including

water, unless otherwise recommended. Bottle-fed babies may be given cooled, boiled tap water in hot weather, but this should be in addition to milk feeds.

When feeding is more established, your baby may need fluids other than milk. Cooled, boiled tap water is the preferred option; some mineral waters are too rich in minerals for babies and bottled water is not sterile. Avoid concentrated fruit juice, cordials, and syrups as they are high in sugar and can damage teeth, even before they appear. You can now drop the lunchtime milk feed. Start with 15ml of water in a cup with a lid and soft spout and increase the amount gradually as you increase the number of meals a day.

INTRODUCING A CUP

It is a good idea to get your baby used to drinking from a cup from about six months,

when you start on solids. If your baby has drunk only from a breast or bottle up until now, changing to a cup may be a challenge and some babies take time to accept the change. Since the object is for your baby to progress from sucking to drinking, open cups or free-flowing feeders are the recommended choices. Many parents, however, opt for a cup with a soft spout, a lid and two handles as this is easier for a young baby than a beaker and as it is a compromise between sucking and ordinary drinking that your baby will probably find it more acceptable. It is important to bear in mind that lidded and spouted cups encourage frequent sipping and have the potential to damage teeth, interfere with oral muscle development and may even have a detrimental effect on speech. Wash her cups in the dishwasher too as lidded cups can also harbour bacteria and it's not uncommon for a baby to happen upon a lost cup hours, or even days, after it was filled, and suck on a drink that is highly likely to be contaminated.

At first, to familiarise your baby with this new method of drinking, try offering some of her usual milk in a cup rather than water.

> ### did you know...
> *Babies are born with a natural store of iron and the mineral is also found in useful amounts in breast and formula milk. By six months of age, however, these iron reserves have largely been used up and even if your baby is breast fed or drinking iron-fortified milk, it is important to include foods rich in the mineral in your baby's diet. Good sources include: red meat, liver, leafy green vegetables, beans and pulses, eggs, fish, dried fruit (especially apricots) and fortified breakfast cereals.*

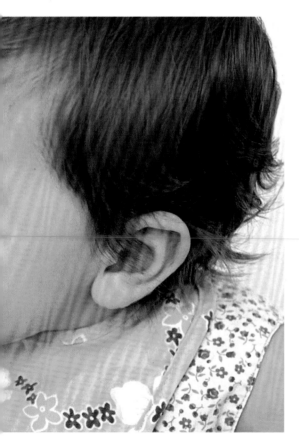

A cup without a spout makes it easier for babies to drink without sipping, which has the potential to damage teeth.

SUPPLEMENTS

The UK Department of Health recommends giving all babies (breast or bottle fed) a liquid supplement of vitamins A, C and D, which is particularly important if your baby is dark-skinned and/or you live in an area with limited sunlight. If your baby is drinking at least 500ml of formula milk or follow-on milk, supplements may not be needed as these milks are already fortified with these vitamins – talk to your health visitor.

FOCUS ON | additives

While the adverse health affects of artificial additives and preservatives on children have always been refuted, a study by the University of Southampton, England, has discovered that certain artificial food colours and preservatives when combined can adversely influence the behaviour of children. Researchers believe the use of additives may help to explain the rise in Attention Deficit Hyperactivity Disorder and parents are advised to cut out some E-numbers and additives altogether.

The colours tested were tartrazine (E102), ponceau 4r (E124), quinoline yellow (E104), sunset yellow (E110), carmoisine (E122), and allura red (E129). It also looked at the preservative sodium benzoate (E211).

COMMERCIAL BABY FOODS

In an ideal world we would all feed our babies nothing but home-prepared food but a combination of homemade with the occasional jar of commercially made baby food is more realistic, manageable and practical for most of us. There are now numerous organic baby food companies making both chilled and frozen meals, many of which are close in quality to home-prepared foods, albeit more costly.

It is important when buying commercial baby foods to read the label carefully and ensure that:

- The ingredients are suitable for your baby's age.
- There are no unwanted additives (see box, left); artificial sweeteners (aspartame, saccharine); sugars (dextrose, sucrose, glucose); salt; and thickeners such as modified starch.
- The product has not passed its best before date.
- The seals are intact.

FOCUS ON | **baby-led weaning**

While current guidelines recommend that weaning begins with puréed food, Gill Rapley, a health visitor for over 25 years, thinks otherwise. She believes feeding babies puréed food is both unnecessary and unnatural and has pioneered what has become known as "Baby-Led Weaning", which centres on babies being in charge of what they eat and how much. The idea is that you present your child with a variety of healthy finger foods or meals made up of solid pieces of food that can be picked up, rather than starting with purées – as long as your baby can sit in a high chair without being propped up.

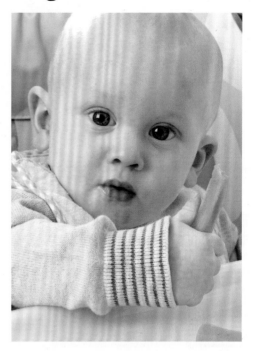

Rapley believes that spoon-feeding puréed food to children could cause health problems later in life and blames the multi-million pound baby food industry for convincing parents that they need to wean their babies on puréed food first. However, offering babies puréed food once they can chew is not only unnecessary, says Rapley, but also could delay chewing skills. In addition, allowing a child to eat as much or as little as she chooses could prevent her from becoming constipated. Constipation can trouble many babies not long after solids are introduced; it's not certain why but it may be down to spoon-fed babies being given more food than they need or with which they can cope.

Ideally, says Rapley, a baby should be fed exclusively breast milk or formula until six months, and then weaned immediately on to finger food as she has found that babies are capable of chewing at this age; they don't need teeth to chew, their gums work well. Ideally, food should be cut into baby fist-sized pieces and should be chip shaped as this provides a baby with a handle with which

to grasp the food. Babies will chew the part sticking out of their fists and drop the rest later on.

Rapley believes that babies allowed to feed themselves tend to become less picky, develop better hand control more quickly and appear to avoid foods to which they were later found to be intolerant. Another advantage is that babies can eat what you're eating and there is no need for puréeing.

Many paediatricians are interested in her findings but some feel that purées could help some babies make the transition between liquid and solid foods more easily. The general feeling is that all babies are different and the remit that one size fits all is inappropriate.

STAGE 2: Increasing The Menu

If your baby is happily eating one "meal" a day (likely to be a few tablespoons) then now is the time to increase the number to two and eventually three in the next few weeks or so. Start adding different foods to familiarise your baby with new tastes and flavour combinations and you will definitely reap the benefits since studies have found that children who have been exposed to a variety of foods from an early age are less likely to be fussy eaters later on in life. Researchers have found that between the ages of six to nine months, children are more receptive to new tastes and textures and their experiences during this period are thought to define their palate in later life.

Do remember that all babies are different – some take to weaning readily, happily accepting new foods, while others take longer. Don't panic or rush things; most importantly, try and ensure mealtimes are as happy and relaxed as possible and not occasions for power games.

COOKING FOR YOUR BABY

It is widely believed that good eating habits are formed early, so it's important at this stage to introduce a wider range of fresh foods, including a greater choice of fruit and vegetables, carbohydrates and proteins.

Carbohydrates include rice, pasta, noodles, potatoes, bread, grains, and oats and other cereals while fish, meat, poultry, full-fat dairy products, well-cooked eggs, pulses (beans and lentils), tofu and meat alternatives are proteins. (For more information, see page 19.)

You'll probably find many of your meals, such as shepherd's pie, thick soups, pasta in tomato sauce or vegetables in cheese sauce are suitable for your baby but avoid adding any seasoning such as salt and hot spices at this stage. Be aware that processed foods may contain sugar, salt, preservatives and milk in various forms such as whey powder.

There are no hard or fast rules as to how much your baby should be eating now but around one to four tablespoons per meal is the general guideline. Try to respond to your baby's appetite; if he is still hungry then you can give him a little more but don't force him to eat if he has eaten only a small amount as this is bound to backfire. At this stage, move on from runny purées to more chunky purées and even mashed or minced foods. (Alternatively, see the information on Baby-led Weaning, page 13.) If your baby spits out any lumps at first, which is not unusual, don't rush this change but gradually increase the texture of his food, making it lumpier and slightly more of a challenge to eat.

Some babies prefer the individual ingredients in their meals to be kept separate so that they can

FOCUS ON | preparing food

The texture of your baby's food should keep pace with his progress. Start by puréeing food to an almost liquid consistency then gradually process for a shorter time in the blender so the food is lumpier. From here, you can mash, mince or finely chop the ingredients.

Chunky purée

Smooth purée

Chopped chicken

log and identify each taste and texture. This makes sense in many ways but obviously the food has to be presented in a form with which your baby can cope.

In many ways, homemade meals are just as convenient and are certainly cheaper than commercially made alternatives since many of your meals will now be suitable for your baby.

Storing and reheating food

It is a good idea to prepare baby meals in bulk and freeze them. If storing meals for later use, cool food as quickly as possible (ideally within 1–2 hours) then place in the fridge. Food can be divided into single portions at this stage then kept in the fridge for up to two days.

If freezing, wrap single portions in freezer cling film or food wrap or place in ice-cube trays. Make sure you label and date the food parcels. When you want to use them, remove from the cling film or ice-cube tray. The safest way to defrost food is to store frozen food in the fridge overnight or use the defrost setting on a microwave or oven.

Reheat foods thoroughly when defrosted. Once piping hot, stir well to remove any hot spots and allow it to cool until it is the right temperature for your baby to eat. If anything is left over, discard it immediately; do not reheat, refreeze or re-use under any circumstances (due to the risk of food poisoning).

ORGANIC FOODS

While you may have to pay a bit more for organic foods, the benefits are numerous. There is good evidence to suggest a connection between pesticide residues and allergies and hyperactivity in children.

Fresh organic produce tends to taste better because it is not intensively grown to absorb excess water and is generally grown in better quality soil and left to ripen for longer. Studies have shown that the lower levels of water in fresh organic produce means that it has higher concentrations of nutrients.

FINGER FOODS

You will probably find your baby loves finger foods. Not only do finger foods help to soothe sore gums and make great snacks, but they also encourage independence through self feeding. Your baby is probably starting to cut a few teeth now and finger foods will allow him to practise chewing and keep him occupied when you are

preparing his food or the family meal.

Make sure fingers foods are not too small or fiddly to hold. Ideally, food should be cut into baby fist-sized, chip-shaped pieces, which makes it easy for a baby to grasp and eat. Do not leave your baby alone when he is feeding to make sure he doesn't choke. Remember to remove any core, skin, seeds or pips from fruit. Try to avoid giving sweet biscuits or rusks as these will only serve to encourage your baby's sweet tooth and lead to weight increase and tooth decay.

Choose from

- Steamed vegetables such as carrot sticks, mangetout, green beans, baby corn or strips of red pepper, chunks of sweet potato, broccoli and asparagus.
- Fruit such as peeled wedges of apple or pear, pieces of banana, mango, melon or peach.
- Large cooked pasta shapes.
- Bread sticks, rice cakes, or fingers of bread, toast or pitta bread.

MILK AND DRINKS

Breast milk, formula or follow-on milk continue to be the main source of nutrients, including iron, for your baby: around 500 to 600ml daily is recommended. However, if you haven't done so already and feeding is established, you now can drop the lunchtime milk feed and provide a feeder cup or beaker of cooled boiled tap water (you may find that he naturally becomes less interested in the bottle and happy to take a cup). At other mealtimes, offer milk after his meal to prevent him becoming too full or preoccupied with the bottle before he has eaten solid foods.

Do not offer cow's, sheep's or goat's milk as a drink, but it can now be used in cooking such as in sauces or desserts.

Steam vegetables until your baby has cut a few teeth and is familiar with finger foods.

FOCUS ON | **allergies**

Statistics show that the number of children with food intolerances and allergies is on the rise, although the number of infants with life-threatening allergies remains relatively small. The prevalence of nut allergy, however, has increased threefold over the last 20 years and affects one in 20 people in the UK.

Many food intolerances and allergies begin in early childhood and the most common allergens are nuts (particularly peanuts), seeds, cow's milk, wheat, gluten, eggs, berries, citrus fruit, tomatoes, sugar and seafood. With a food intolerance, the body struggles to digest a particular food. A food intolerance can develop over a period of time – even into adulthood. With a food allergy, the immune system has an immediate adverse reaction to a particular food, or trigger. Allergic reaction is potentially serious, but it is also far more rare than a food intolerance. Intolerances can be difficult to detect since symptoms are wide ranging, including colic, upset tummy, rashes and hyperactivity to asthma and eczema.
A severe allergic reaction, or anaphylactic shock, can begin with symptoms such as generalised rash and flushed appearance, but can quickly develop into swelling of the face and mouth, difficulty swallowing and result in severe breathing difficulties. Anaphylaxis needs urgent medical attention; so call an ambulance if you notice any of the symptoms.

It is recommended that common allergenic foods are introduced into the diet gradually and one at a time, which allows you to monitor any adverse reaction.

Children are more susceptible than adults to food intolerance because they have immature digestive and immune systems. Intolerances and allergies both tend to run in families. Babies who face the highest risk of nut allergy, for example, are those whose immediate families suffer from a nut allergy or other allergic conditions such as asthma, eczema and hay fever (known as "atopic" allergy). Children who have one parent with an allergy carry a 30 per cent risk of developing a condition, but having two such parents pushes the risk up to 70 per cent. It is recommended that babies at risk should not be given nuts and nut-related products until the age of three, and that parents try to be vigilant when reading food labels as just a small quantity of nuts in a product can cause a severe reaction.

There is no need to avoid nuts or nut products, if there are no cases of intolerances or allergies within the family, particularly as they are highly nutritious. However, make sure they are ground, finely chopped or crushed if giving them to young children, as they are a choking risk.

If there is a history of food allergies in the family or indeed hay fever, eczema and asthma, please consult your doctor or health visitor as to dietary restrictions.

Some allergies can be helped by eating a healthy, well-balanced diet that is low in sugar and additives. A diet that contains plenty of different types of fruits and vegetables has been shown to play a preventative role for those suffering from asthma, for example.

Note
All recipes containing nuts and seeds in the recipe section are highlighted.

STAGE 3: Three Meals A Day

If your baby is happily eating the meals you are giving her, from around the age of seven to nine months, you can start to increase the number of solid feeds from two to three, if you have not done so already. Again introduce new foods gradually but try to make sure your baby is eating a range of foods to get a good balance of nutrients, particularly iron (see page 11). You will probably find that many family meals are suitable but avoid chilli, other hot spices and seasoning. Mashed, minced or finely chopped foods will encourage your baby to chew.

? Is your baby eating enough

At around 8-9 months, your baby will start to enjoy three meals a day and will benefit from a varied diet based on the following:

✓ 3-4 servings a day of starchy carbohydrate foods such as bread, pasta, rice, potatoes and breakfast cereals.

✓ 2-3 servings a day of meat, fish, poultry, beans, pulses, eggs and dairy products.

✓ 3-4 servings a day of fruit and vegetables.

VEGETARIAN BABIES

With a little planning and attention, a vegetarian diet can provide all the nutrients a baby needs for growth and development. As with any diet, variety is the key. Make sure you provide protein from a variety of sources including nuts (if there is no sign of an allergy within the family), seeds, eggs, dairy products, beans and pulses, including lentils, tofu, and combine with vitamin C-rich fruit and vegetables to aid iron absorption. A meat-free diet is naturally high in fibre, too much of which may result in an upset stomach, low energy intake and interfere with the absorption of iron, zinc and copper. For these reasons, avoid giving your baby, at least when very young, large quantities of brown rice, wholegrain bread or wholemeal pasta. Try to make pulses and beans a significant part of your baby's diet; they are an important source of iron and also make a great base for many savoury dishes such as soups, stews and dips. Make sure your baby is getting enough B vitamins, and iron and zinc, in particular (see page 21).

WHAT BABIES NEED

Babies grow a lot in the first year and have high energy requirements for their size. Aim to provide a good balance of especially fresh foods, but at this stage also think about how your baby's diet pans out over a week rather than on a daily basis: eating patterns can be erratic in infants, and after all you are still in the relatively early stages of weaning.

Carbohydrate/starchy foods (about 3-4 servings a day)

The following are an excellent source of energy, vitamins, minerals and fibre (while a diet rich in fibre is perfect for adults, avoid giving too many high-fibre foods to babies as they find them difficult to digest and they can upset the digestive system):

- Sugar-free breakfast cereals and oats
- Pasta and noodles
- Rice
- Bread
- Potatoes

Protein foods (about 2-3 servings a day)

The following provide a good source of protein, essential for growth and repair in the body. Offer a combination of protein foods to get a good mix of essential amino acids:

- Fish
- Tofu
- Meat and poultry
- Meat alternatives
- Well-cooked eggs
- Full-fat cheese (grated or cubed)
- Beans and pulses
- Yogurt or fromage frais

Milk

Milk provides protein, vitamins and minerals, particularly calcium for strong teeth and bones. Cow's milk can be used in cooking from six months but not given as a drink until your child is one year old, when full-fat milk can be introduced. Half-fat milk is suitable from two years, while skimmed milk is not recommended until five years of age, as it does not provide the energy a growing child requires.

Fruit and vegetables (3-4 or more servings a day)

Fresh, frozen, canned and dried fruit and vegetables are an essential part of a baby's diet. They make ideal first foods and provide rich amounts of vitamins, particularly vitamin C, minerals and fibre. Foods containing vitamin C (good for immune system, hair, skin and nails) should be included in meals as they assist the absorption of iron. Try to provide your baby with a variety of fresh produce. The following are all suitable but the list is far from exhaustive:

- Peeled apple
- Banana
- Mango
- Apricots
- Peaches and nectarines
- Melon
- Strawberries
- Carrot
- Broccoli
- Green beans
- Peas
- Pepper
- Mangetout

FOODS TO AVOID IN EARLY CHILDHOOD

Whole nuts should not be given to children under five because of the risk of choking. However, all foods containing nuts are to be avoided if there is a history of food allergies within the immediate family (see page 17). Flaked, finely chopped nuts or peanut butter are suitable from six months of age if there is no history of allergies.

Sugar is high in calories, nutritionally poor and will spoil a child's appetite. It also leads to tooth decay and, if eaten in excess, may lead to obesity. Sugary foods often include a fair amount of fat — just think of doughnuts, biscuits and cakes.

Honey is a sugary food and causes similar health problems. It also very occasionally contains a bacterium that has been known to cause infant botulism. For this reason, honey is not recommended for babies under one year (after this age the intestines are sufficiently mature to prevent the bacteria growing).

Cow's, sheep's or goat's milk are not recommended as a drink for babies under one year as they do not contain sufficient iron and other nutrients needed by infants.. However, from six months of age, these milks can be mixed into a baby's cooked dishes such a cheese sauces, or poured over breakfast cereals.

Eggs should be cooked until both the white and yolk are solid. Raw or partially cooked eggs can be a source of salmonella, which can cause food poisoning, particularly in vulnerable babies.

Salt can be harmful to a baby's immature kidneys if added to food. Up to seven months of age, babies should have less than 1g salt a day; from seven to 12 months 1g a day is the maximum recommended amount. Children between the ages of one and three years should have no more than 2g salt a day. Naturally salty foods such as bacon, cheese, stock, yeast extract also should be limited. Be aware that milk contains salt, so babies are getting some even when not eating many weaning foods.

Shellfish, such as prawns and mussels due to the slight risk of food poisoning.

Marlin, shark and swordfish have been found to contain significant amounts of mercury and it is recommended that you don't include these fish in a child's diet as the mercury can affect the developing nervous system.

Foods high in saturated fat can be harmful to a child's health, increasing the risk of heart problems in later life as well as Type 2 diabetes. Avoid giving too many fatty foods such as butter, cheese, margarine, fatty meat and meat products, biscuits, pastry and cakes. Do not, however, avoid fats altogether — they are needed for nerve development. Instead, ensure your baby eats foods rich in omega-3 and omega-6 fatty acids such as oily fish and vegetable oils.

- B12: eggs, cheese, textured vegetable protein, fortified foods such as breakfast cereals and yeast extract.
- Iron: beans, lentils, leafy green vegetables, dairy products, fortified breakfast cereals, dried fruit, brown rice and wholegrain bread.
- Zinc: nuts, seeds, dairy products, beans, lentils, whole grains and yeast extract.

SELF-FEEDING

Lots of babies like to feed themselves from an early age and you may find that your baby tries to grab her feeding spoon from you. This growing sense of independence is no bad thing and also encourages good hand/eye coordination, while learning to bite and chew helps with speech development. Let her have her own spoon while you continue feeding with a second one – things may get messy but that's half the fun!

It may take a few months (or years!) for your baby to become proficient at feeding herself with a spoon and most of the meals may end up on the floor or smeared over the highchair rather than in her mouth. Prepare for the mess by putting a plastic sheet or newspaper on the floor and remaining calm about any mishaps. You can help by offering foods that are easy to scoop up on a spoon like mashed potato, thick cottage cheese, cooked rice and cereal. Finger foods (see page 16) and meals cut into manageable chunks rather than mashed are easier to pick up and may ease any frustration. The more your baby is allowed to use her hands, the sooner she is likely to become more accomplished with a spoon. This also allows her to take an active part in mealtimes and she'll begin to enjoy being involved.

BREAKFAST

LUNCH

	BREAKFAST	Mid Morning Milk (every day)	LUNCH	Mid Afternoon Milk (every day)
MONDAY	Porridge with Apricot Purée 61		Sardines on Toast Fingers 72	
TUESDAY	Egg Cups 65		Tomato & Tuna Gnocchi 105	
WEDNESDAY	Date & Vanilla Breakfast Yoghurt 57		Baked Potato with Humous & Roasted Red Pepper filling 80	
THURSDAY	Home-made Baked Beans 78 with toast		Ham & Pea Penne 120	
FRIDAY	Golden Crunch 59		Sweet Potato Bake 102	
SATURDAY	Eggy Bread 64		Muffin Pizzas 87 and vegetable sticks	
SUNDAY	Banana & Strawberry Smoothie 56 with toast and a well-cooked poached egg		Plaice with Roasted Tomatoes 107	

DINNER

Meaty Paella 118

Macaroni & Leek Cheese 94

Vegetable Soup with Chicken Dumplings
111

Salmon Fingers with Sweet Potato Chips
109

Turkey Fricassée 117

Meat Balls with Tomato Sauce 124
and rice

Spaghetti with Roasted Butternut Squash
96

DESSERTS

Apple & Cinnamon Compote 133

Banana & Maple Yogurt Ice 130

Quick Summer Pudding 132

Fruit Yogurt Swirls 128

Mango Fool 129

Peach Crumbles 136

Strawberry Sundae 131

Bedtime Milk (every day)

STAGE 4: **Family Meals**

As your baby approaches his first birthday, there are fewer occasions when a specially prepared meal is necessary. He can now enjoy most of the foods as the rest of the family with a few exceptions. Joining in with family meals is one way to learn good eating habits as these are shaped and honed when young. It is also more convenient as there is no need to prepare separate meals. In the selection of recipes, there are many, which both you and your baby will enjoy. When you won't be eating together, consider preparing meals (without seasoning) in bulk and freezing them in baby-sized portions for future use but make sure you defrost and reheat the meals thoroughly before serving. Commercially made baby foods also have their place but don't let them replace homemade meals altogether.

KEEPING PACE WITH YOUR BABY

Coarsely mash, finely chop, grate or mince meals, as this will help your baby to practise chewing skills, benefit teeth and aid speech development. It may take a while for your baby to accept foods with a coarser texture but persist, taking things slowly and being as encouraging and positive as possible.

Babies thrive on routine and because their energy requirements are high in relation to the size, they require three small meals a day. If convenient, give the main meal of the day at lunchtime when your bay is alert and not feeling too grouchy. If your baby has started to crawl or is going through a growth spurt, he also may need a couple of healthy snacks between meals to keep energy levels sufficiently high. Unsurprisingly, sugary, salty, high-fat and highly processed snacks are not recommended, as they are low in nutrients and high in calories.

Never force your baby to eat as this will only serve to put him off altogether. If you are worried he is not eating enough, talk to your health visitor who will look at your baby's growth chart and weight and will monitor progress; you may well find that your fears are ungrounded and he is continuing to progress well. If he seems active and lively then he is likely to be getting enough energy from what

SNACKS TO TRY

- Hard-boiled egg

- Fingers of bread or toast

- Rice cakes with yeast extract

- Pitta bread with hummus

- Cheese sticks or grated cheese

- Vegetable sticks, cooked or raw

- Slices or large cubes of fruit

- Pieces of dry, sugar-free cereal

- Yoghurt or fromage frais

- Dried fruit

- Toast with nut butter (as long as there is no family history of nut allergy)

- Breadsticks with dip

- Fingers of cooked chicken

he is eating. Milk is also considered a food rather than a drink so if your baby is drinking 500 to 600ml a day then he will be getting a range of important nutrients but it should not be viewed as a meal replacement.

TROUBLE-FREE MEALTIMES

Your baby is unlikely to love every meal he is given but don't force him to eat if he turns his nose up. Omit the same food or meal for a few days then try offering it again – maybe in a different way this time. Teething and general wellbeing can undoubtedly influence a baby's eating habits, which many parents will attest can frustratingly change on almost a daily basis!

At this stage, many babies also show an increasing desire for independence and may become choosier about what they eat. If you remain calm, the less likely your baby is going to use eating as a time to test your patience and the more harmonious mealtimes will be; sometimes this may be easier said than done but it's well worth a try!

Your baby will probably now be sitting in a high chair or a baby seat attached to the dining table, enabling him to join in with family meals. Self-feeding is an important stage in a baby's development as it helps hand/eye coordination and encourages independence. Give your baby food with a fairly stiff consistency in a non-slip plastic bowl. Finger foods are also perfect for practising self-feeding but you may find that all meals are eaten with his hands at first and this is no bad thing.

MILK

Milk remains an important source of nutrients in your baby's diet for the first year and for many years beyond this; 500–600ml is recommended a day, although some of this amount can be provided by milky puddings and sauces or poured over breakfast cereals. Avoid giving cow's, sheep's or goat's milk as a drink until your baby is one year old, opting instead for breast, formula or follow-on milk instead. Continuing to breastfeed ensures that your baby gets milk designed for his needs, so giving other milk may not be needed. If your baby becomes ill and loses his appetite, breastfeeding can keep him well nourished, giving him important antibodies to tackle bugs, as well as comforting him until he feels better.

OTHER DRINKS

If you haven't done so by now, try weaning your baby off the bottle by introducing a beaker or trainer cup with two handles, so he can take sips of water or very diluted fresh fruit juice during mealtimes. Drinks from a cup are said to be better for speech development and for his developing teeth. Tea, coffee, fizzy drinks, sugary fruit drinks, including low-sugar varieties, are not intended for babies and are best avoided.

From one year

Many babies happily enjoy family meals by their first birthdays. However, just as you think you have weaning in the bag, it is not uncommon for a child to become more fussy or faddy about food around this age, having happily wolfed down everything that was offered previously. This is perfectly normal and it's good to remember that this is just a stage your toddler is going through and it will not have a long-term detrimental affect on health. Stick to your guns and continue to offer as varied a diet as possible, encompassing a wide range of colours, textures and flavours. Look at what your toddler eats over a week rather than on a daily basis, and you may find that overall she is eating a good varied diet, despite the occasional meal that remains largely uneaten or the day when she only wants to eat peanut butter sandwiches. Most importantly, don't panic if your toddler goes through periods of not eating well; you'll no doubt find that she is eating what she needs. Energy requirements increase from years one to three as your toddler continues to grow and becomes more active.

FOCUS ON | **sugar and sweets**

Most children naturally have a sweet tooth (breast milk and formula milk is sweet, for starters and babies need this as they feed little and often) but hold off giving your child sugary foods as long as feasible as sugar cravings are hard to break. Foods made from refined sugar are high in calories, nutritionally poor, will spoil a child's appetite as well as lead to tooth decay; what's more, sugary foods often include a fair amount of fat – just think of doughnuts, biscuits and cakes.

Nevertheless, an outright sugar ban can backfire, making sweets even more desirable! It may be preferential to avoid over-processed sugary, artificially coloured confections rather than cutting out sugar altogether. Don't resort to foods that replace sugar with artificial sweeteners, as they have been found to cause digestive problems if eaten in large quantities and in the long-term are no better than the refined alternative.

SNACKS TO TRY

- Hard-boiled egg with toast fingers

- Sticks of cheese with apple slices and oatcake

- Toasted cheese muffin

- Chunks of melon with ham

- Tuna mayonnaise with toasted tortilla triangles

- Humous and breadsticks

- Rice cake with nut butter

- Mashed banana sandwich

- Pitta bread with yeast extract and carrot sticks

- Good-quality meatballs with halved cherry tomatoes

- Dried apple rings

- Toasted fruit muffin or teacake

- Natural yogurt with mango

- Slice of fruit cake

- Fruit scone

- Chunks of fresh fruit

- Raisins or chopped dried fruit

Although the need for good-quality protein is much the same (two or three servings a day), there is an increased need for all vitamins and minerals, except vitamin D, which is supplied by exposure to sunlight.

KEEP IT HEALTHY

The term "balanced diet" can intimidate even the most nutritionally aware parent, but as long as your child eats a good mix of foods on a regular basis then she will get all the nutrients she needs.

A diet high in fibre and low in fat remains unsuitable for children of this age, as this may preclude youngsters being able to obtain all the energy and nutrients they require. Additionally,

WHAT TODDLERS NEED

The dietary habits of later life are often determined by eating patterns that develop in the early years. If your toddler is picky about her food, as many are, don't be tempted to take the easy option and indulge all her whims. Encourage her to eat as varied a diet as possible.

Carbohydrate/starchy foods
(4–5 servings a day)

Bread, cereals, pasta, rice and potatoes are excellent sources of energy, fibre, vitamins and minerals. Carbohydrates should form the main part of every meal but bear in mind that toddlers find it difficult to digest large amounts of high-fibre foods such as wholemeal bread and brown rice, so try providing a combination of white and brown carbohydrate foods. If making a fruit crumble, for instance, combine white and wholemeal flour for the topping, and you could also follow this principle if making biscuits, cakes and bread.

Potatoes provide useful amounts of vitamin C, which is found mainly just under the skin so avoid peeling them if you can. Thin-skinned potatoes can simply be scrubbed and jacket potatoes are also a good source of nutrients. Add sweet potato, swede or parsnip to mashed potato to boost its nutritional value.

Dairy products

Full-fat milk, cheese, yoghurt and fromage frais provide protein for growth and development, calcium for teeth and, together with vitamin D, helps make bones and teeth stronger. Childhood is a crucial time for tooth and bone development and continues to influence bone health in adulthood.

Crème fraîche, fromage frais and thick natural yoghurt make useful alternatives to cream in cooking and are also lower in fat; use them in sauces, soups, pies – both sweet and savoury. (See Milk below.)

Protein foods
(2–3 servings a day)

Meat, poultry, fish, eggs and pulses provide rich amounts of vitamins and minerals and are essential for your toddler's growth and development. If she is vegetarian, plan to give her a good mix of protein foods including beans, lentils, tofu, nuts and eggs.

Oily fish is the richest source of omega-3 essential fatty acids, which have been found to benefit the brain, eyes and skin. Research has also shown a correlation between fatty acid levels in children and their intellectual and behavioural performance as youngsters (see page 35). You can give boys up to four servings a week of oily fish including tuna (canned is not as rich in omega-3 as fresh), salmon, mackerel, herring, sardines, pilchards and trout and girls up to two portions. Omega-3 is also found in non-fish sources such as fortified eggs, drinks and cereals, walnuts, linseeds, rapeseed, pumpkin seeds and soya beans.

Red meat and liver are rich in iron but cut off any excess fat. Lean, good-quality mince can be transformed into homemade burgers and kofta, or used as a base for pastry or potato-topped pies, pasta sauces and in stir-fries.

Fruit and vegetables
(5 servings a day)

Whether fresh, frozen, canned, dried or juiced, fruit and vegetables provide a whole host of vitamins and minerals, especially vitamin C, that are vital for good health. A minimum of five portions a day is recommended and a serving for a toddler is one satsuma, half an apple or banana, five grapes, a floret of broccoli, a dessertspoon of peas or carrots or one tomato. A small glass of fresh fruit juice also counts.

It probably won't come as much of a surprise to find out that most children do not eat enough fresh produce, and the majority of parents will have experienced the struggle to get their children to eat up their greens.

Try presenting fruit and vegetables in different ways. For example, many children turn their nose up at cooked vegetables, but will happily eat them raw, including sticks of cucumber, carrot and red pepper. Vegetables sticks are good for dunking into dips so serve them with nutritious guacamole or humous (see pages 16 and 70) and you'll double the health benefits. Alternatively incorporate vegetables into fritters or rosti, or if the going gets really tough, disguise puréed vegetables into sauces, stews, soups and pies. A love of fruit is perhaps easier to encourage but again maintain the interest with different types and presenting them in various ways.

a diet high in fibre will also reduce the amount of minerals absorbed, including valuable iron and calcium. Likewise, children need a certain amount of fat for normal growth and development. Not all fat is bad and it has an important role to play in transporting vitamins A, D, E and K through the body. Unsaturated fat is found in vegetables oils, oily fish and soft margarine and is an important contributor to good health.

Try to provide a good mix of high-energy, nutrient dense foods based on the food groups discussed on these pages on a daily basis (obviously, the range of foods eaten will vary depending on special diets, eating preferences and the presence of food intolerances):

SNACKS

Toddlers have high energy requirements for their size, consequently small, frequent meals, plus two to three healthy snacks are necessary for a child of this age, who does not have a large enough stomach to cope with three large meals a day. You'll probably find that your child will need a snack mid morning, mid afternoon and maybe pre-bedtime. Some children love to graze, take advantage of this by offering healthy snacks, turning them into mini-meals rather than opting for sugary, salty or fatty processed foods. However, it's also important for children to enjoy main meals and constant snacking can deter them from doing this.

MILK

Whole cow's, sheep's or goat's milk can be given to children over the age of 12 months as a main drink. Your child still requires about 500 to 600ml milk a day, although some of this can be provided by milky puddings and sauces, or poured over breakfast cereals. Aim for your child to give up a bottle by one year old and to move on to a cup or beaker of milk.

While you may still be breastfeeding, it is no longer necessary to offer formula or follow-on milk, although you can continue to do so if you

	BREAKFAST	Breakfast Milk	LUNCH
MONDAY	Golden Crunch 59 with milk and chopped apple		Miso Noodle Soup 85
TUESDAY	Eggy Bread 64 and Home-made Baked Beans 78		Mexican Rice 100
WEDNESDAY	Porridge with Apricot Purée 61		Sardines on Toast Fingers 72
THURSDAY	Boiled egg and Homemade Baked Beans 78		Halloumi & Pitta Salad 77
FRIDAY	Tomato & Egg Scramble 63		Tuna Tortilla Melt 92
SATURDAY	Mini Banana Pancakes 66		Baby Falafel Burgers 89
SUNDAY	Banana & Strawberry Smoothie 56 with Potato Cakes with Beans 67	Milk in smoothie	Mozzarella Tortilla Parcel 90

DINNER

Sausage & Potato Roast 119

Barbecue Chicken with Coleslaw 112

Creamy Broccoli Pasta Bake 97

Pork with Fruity Couscous 121

Lentil Dahl 104
with rice

Turkey Fricassée 117

Creamy Fish Pie 108

DESSERTS

Apple and Plum Flapjack Pie 141

Carrot Cake Square 138

Mixed Fruit Compote 133
with fromage frais

Strawberry Yogurt Ice 131

Mango Fool 129

Apple & Cinnamon Compote 133
with ice cream

Lemon Sponge Pudding 139

Bedtime Milk (every day)

feel your child is not eating well or you are concerned that she is not getting the range of nutrients needed. Semi-skimmed can be introduced after your child is two, as long as she is eating well. Skimmed milk is not recommended for children under five years of age, as it does not provide enough energy and vitamin A for a growing child.

FOCUS ON iron

Iron deficiency is not uncommon in children so try to give a food or drink rich in vitamin C, such as fruit juice or vegetables, at the same time as an iron-rich food as this will help the absorption of this mineral.

Don't give tea and coffee to young children, especially at mealtimes; not only do they contain caffeine but they interfere with the amount of iron absorption. As iron is more difficult to absorb from non-meat sources, if your child is vegetarian opt to give her foods containing iron everyday such as beans, lentils, green leafy vegetables, dried fruit, particularly apricots, raisins and sultanas, as well as fortified breakfast cereals.

DRINKS

Water is always the best drink option for children but diluted fresh fruit juice provides vitamin C and if served alongside a meal containing iron can help absorption of this mineral. However, even fruit juice contains natural sugars, so avoid giving it to your child other than at mealtimes to prevent damage to her teeth, since the longer a sugary drink is in contact with teeth, the more damage it can do.

Fruit squash, fizzy drinks and those containing caffeine are best avoided as they are high in sugar, a source of empty calories and nutritionally poor. They also fill children up, affecting their appetite for meals. Water is the best option between meals.

SUPPLEMENTS

It is recommended that between the ages of one to five years, a liquid supplement of vitamin A, C and D should be given unless your infant is eating a good varied diet containing these nutrients and exposure to sunlight is sufficient. These should be continued until your child is five if she is a poor eater or does not have much exposure to sunlight.

From Two Years

As your toddler becomes more active, the more calories he will require to give him the energy needed. Encourage your child to eat a variety of foods so he gets a wide range of nutrients (see Keep it Healthy, page 27).

Work on establishing a regular eating pattern based on three meals plus two to three snacks a day. Some children continue to dislike lumps in their food, so chopping or mincing food may make it more acceptable. Alternatively, finger foods are a great way of encouraging your toddler to chew foods and to enjoy those with a coarser texture.

Your toddler may now attend nursery or playgroup and this can come with its own challenges and peer pressure. You may be fortunate to find one that makes its own healthy lunches and snacks, but standards can vary, so talk to other parents and get some feedback about meals. Some nurseries are open to parents providing their own packed lunches, drinks and snacks and this may be a welcome option.

GOOD EATING HABITS

Your child is becoming increasingly aware of the world around him and with this comes a new sense of independence and free will, with both its positive and not so positive side effects, but studies show parents who instil good eating habits from an early age are likely to see the benefits in the long-term. Points to consider include:

- Don't get hung up on good eating manners just yet; there's plenty of time for that. Your toddler will continue to make a mess when he eats – crumbs become a way of life! While ideally you would like him to eat with a fork or spoon, fingers or hands will continue to be much in use.
- While it's not always feasible for the whole family to eat together, you will reap the benefits when you do, even if you manage communal mealtimes only at weekends. Eating together encourages chatter and discussion between parents and children and gets them away from the TV screen. Children also learn good eating habits from their parents so make sure you eat up your greens!
- Be patient and persevere. If you manage to persuade your child to try even a mouthful of food you are making progress, and he may find he likes it after all. Research shows that children acquire a taste for foods over time and it takes an average of 10 "tastes" for a child to accept new foods. The theory is that if a parents can persuade their child to eat just one mouthful of carrots on 10 occasions, he will learn to like them.
- Attempts to encourage your child to eat healthy foods can be helped if you make food

exciting – this doesn't mean that you have to spend hours making faces out of ingredients but bear in mind different colours, textures and shapes when planning a meal. Interesting or colourful plates, bibs, cutlery and mats can also make a difference, as can introducing a theme. Steamed vegetables are brighter in colour than boiled, while fresh veg have an appealing crunchy texture. Imaginative and attractive presentation can usually make the difference between a child eating or refusing a meal.

- Many parents fall into the trap of believing children prefer bland or so-called "children's food". In fact, a study has found that children like stronger flavours than once thought and will happily try curries, stir-fries, chilli and the like, if encouraged.
- Even if you have managed to keep your child away from sugar until now, it becomes increasingly tricky as he becomes older, interacts with other children, and is more aware of children-oriented brands with their brightly coloured cartoon character

packaging. Everything is moderation seems to work for most parents but opt for the ones with the least amount of colours, additives and preservatives!

- One of the best ways to get your child interested in food is to teach him to cook or at least become involved in the preparation of a meal, even if it's as simple as a quick stir of a sauce or pouring some cereal into a bowl.
- Similarly, get your child involved in food shopping; allow him to choose from healthy options, weigh fresh produce or unpack.

FUSSY EATERS

All children go through stages of picky eating and appetites can be equally unpredictable – a fact confirmed by the majority of parents. But how do you encourage your child to eat what he is given and what do you do if he refuses to eat? Perhaps predictably there are no easy answers but the following tips should help you with those more challenging times:

- Forcing your child to eat is a no-win situation for the both of you. Conflict and tension serve only to make the situation more difficult and may lead to your child using mealtimes as a way of seeking attention. It can be incredibly frustrating if your child does not eat a meal that you have lovingly prepared but children are remarkably clever at picking up on the anxieties of their parents and may well tune into your own frustrations about their not eating.
- Gently coax or offer plenty of encouragement to try just a mouthful or a "no thank you bite"; sometimes this is enough for him to be persuaded to eat the rest of the meal.
- Praise your child as much as possible, even if he eats just the one mouthful.
- If encouragement and coaxing don't work take the food away but don't offer an alternative, however hard this may be. It's important that a child gets used to eating what he is given and does not expect alternatives if he doesn't like the first option.
- Don't make portions too large, as this can be off-putting for a child – you can always give him seconds if a meal is eaten up.
- Peer pressure can work both ways: ask a friend of your child's who you know to be a good eater to come to tea. Children often learn by example and if they see their peers eating up it may well encourage them to do the same.
- Making eating fun: picnics, even if it is only a cloth arranged on the floor, or a theme based on a favourite game or book can be a real winner.

- Sticker charts can be unbelievably successful and are a simple way of encouraging children to try new foods, especially unfamiliar fruit and vegetables.
- It may be easier said than done, but don't fall into the trap of bribing your child with a pudding or sweets.
- Compromise is sometimes the only option. Combine foods you know your child likes with ones previously untried or previously rejected; you may find that new combinations are enough to encourage your child to try new things.

WEIGHT ISSUES

The incidence of obesity in many parts of the world is rising, and unfortunately children are not immune from what is being called an epidemic.

In the UK, for example, the prevalence of obesity has increased markedly among both adults and children since the mid 1990s. In 1995, 10 per cent of primary school age boys and 12 per cent of girls were obese. Figures released in 2012/13 showed that 9.3 per cent of children aged 4–5 years were obese and another 13 per cent were overweight. This figure rose for 10–11 year olds, with 18.9 per cent being obese and a further 14.4 per cent overweight. Overall the obesity rates are about one per cent higher in boys than girls. It is also now known that obese mothers tend to have babies who become obese.

Many experts put the rise in obesity down to the growing presence of fast-food outlets, advertising and the overwhelming choice of cakes, biscuits, sweets, ice cream, crisps, snacks and fizzy drinks in shops. While this hasn't helped the situation, lifestyle also has a role to play: with the ever-increasing popularity of computer games and television, children are becoming less and less physically active, so are not burning the calories they have consumed.

However, there could be other reasons for a child being overweight that are not as simple as over-eating or inactivity, so it's advisable to consult your doctor before putting your child on any type of diet, which could restrict nutritional intake if not handled correctly. Most fat babies will start to slim down when they begin to crawl or walk and become normal-weight toddlers, but a few remain overweight. The best way to prevent a child becoming fat is to breastfeed exclusively for six months and to teach good eating habits early on; prevention is much easier than cure. Try to stick to a routine of three meals a day plus two

to three healthy snacks. Many children are grazers, but constant nibbling makes them less likely to enjoy a proper meal. Young children should not be put on weight-reduction diets unless advised by a doctor. However, developing a healthy family approach to food and exercise is important in weight management.

MILK

If your child eats well and has a varied, balanced diet then it is possible, but not necessary, to switch to half-fat milk after two years of age.

Skimmed milk, however, is not recommended before five years, as it does not provide sufficient energy and nutrients for your growing child.

DRINKS

Many children don't drink enough and will happily go for hours without drinking. Proper hydration helps the brain function at its best, so ensure your child drinks plenty of water, not dehydrating fizzy, sugary drinks. Dehydration affects concentration as well as the transportation of nutrients around the body.

	BREAKFAST	LUNCH
MONDAY	Seedy Banana Breakfast 60	Quick & Easy Sausage Rolls 93 with Vegetable Fingers 101
TUESDAY	Egg Cups 65	Mexican Rice 100
WEDNESDAY	Porridge with Apricot Purée 61	Pea Soup 84 with bread
THURSDAY	Ham & Egg Cups 64 with grilled tomatoes	Mini Quiches 88 with Country Garden Salad 76
FRIDAY	Golden Crunch 59 with milk and chopped strawberries	Baby Falafel Burgers 89
SATURDAY	Date & Vanilla Breakfast Yogurt 57 with toast and Three-nut Butter 58	Vegetable Fingers 101 with steamed vegetables
SUNDAY	Breakfast Omelette 62 and beans	Roasted Red Pesto Chicken 114

DINNER

Pesto & Pea Risotto 99

Ham & Pea Penne 120

Turkey Patties with Pineapple Relish 116

Tomato & Tuna Gnocchi 105

Plaice with Roasted Tomatoes 107

Chinese Beef with Noodles 127

Salmon Frittata 110

DESSERTS

Merry Berry Cobbler 140

Oat Cookie 135
with fruit

Sticky Date Cake 137

Fruit Yogurt Swirls 128

Peach Crumbles 136

Quick Summer Pudding 132

Sticky Date Cake 137

Bedtime Milk (every day)

ABOUT THE RECIPES

The recipes have been designed to appeal to children of all ages and each comes with a recommended age, which relates to the suitability of the ingredients used. All First Foods are suitable for babies from six months. Treat these age recommendations as a general guide since babies progress at different rates. Some may start on purées and then progress to more complex dishes in a few weeks, while others take a bit longer. You know your baby best, so please do not feed him something before you think he is ready, but try to ensure he eats some iron-rich foods (see page 11) from six months, since stores of the mineral deplete from this age.

Use your common sense to serve the dish best suited to your baby's stage of development – puréed, mashed, minced or chopped.

Many of the main meals have been created for a family of four – two children, two adults – to eat together but storing suggestions are given if you wish to freeze or chill portions for future serving. Some of the recipes contain added sweeteners but the amount per portion is minimal.

 number of portions or servings

 suggestions for accompaniments

 suitable to eat from this age

RECIPES

These recipes make excellent starter meals for your baby – all are suitable from the age of six months. They have been intentionally kept very simple to enable your baby to try a "taster" of solids and to become gradually accustomed to eating.

To begin with, there are a selection of single-ingredient – fruit or vegetable – purées. These are followed by mixed ingredient purées, ranging from simple vegetable and fruit combinations to those incorporating pasta and grains. The single ingredient purées also can be combined to introduce variation. There's also a range of dessert purées.

The portion sizes are a very rough guide and you will probably find that your baby will only eat a few teaspoons (if that) at first. The remainder – not leftovers – can be stored in the fridge for a day or you could make double the quantity and freeze in individual portions.

BABY RICE

There are many commercial versions of baby rice in the shops but it's just as easy to make your own. Mix with breast milk or formula milk to make a smooth, thin purée. Baby rice can also be used as a base to mix with fruit and vegetable purées.

 **makes 4–7 portions**

INGREDIENTS

25g white short-grain
   rice

1 Put the rice in a sieve and rinse under cold running water. Transfer to a saucepan and add enough cold water to cover. Bring to the boil, stir, then reduce the heat.

2 Cover the pan with a lid and simmer for 10 to 15 minutes until the water has been absorbed and the grains are very tender.

3 Purée the rice in a blender with sufficient breast or formula milk to make a smooth, runny purée.

STORAGE TIP
Baby rice is suitable for freezing but make sure it has completely defrosted and is heated through until piping hot to avoid any risk of contamination. Check the temperature before serving.

BANANA PURÉE

This makes a perfect first food and is simple to prepare. Make sure you use a very ripe banana as this will be much easier on your baby's digestive system.

Remove the skin and put the banana in a bowl. Mash with a fork until smooth as possible. Add a little boiled water or breast or formula milk to make a thin purée, if necessary.

STORAGE TIP
Unsuitable for freezing

makes 1 portion

INGREDIENTS

½ banana

APPLE PURÉE

Apple goes well with baby rice – either home-made or shop-bought – and when your baby is ready is excellent combined with puréed meat and vegetables.

1 Wash, peel, core and finely chop the apple. Put the apple in a saucepan with the water and bring to the boil. Reduce the heat and simmer, half-covered, for 5–8 minutes until tender.

2 Transfer the apple to a blender and purée until smooth, adding a little of the cooking water if necessary.

makes 2–3 portions

INGREDIENTS

1 dessert apple
2 tbsp water

VARIATION
Pear can be prepared in the same way as apple. It is an excellent first food, particularly as it is one of the least allergenic of foods. If the pear is nice and ripe then it can simply be peeled, cored and mashed.

MELON PURÉE

Any variety of melon can be given uncooked to your baby but make sure it is ripe and juicy. Wash the skin of the melon before cutting into it. It may be necessary to steam the melon if it's not entirely ripe.

 **makes 1 portion**

INGREDIENTS

1 small wedge melon

Scoop out the seeds from the melon then cut away the flesh from the skin. Purée to a smooth consistency – it's unlikely you will need to add any water as melon has a high water content.

VARIATION
Mango and papaya also make great first foods, simply prepare as above.

PREPARATION TIP
If the melon is ripe enough, you will probably be able to mash it with a fork or pass through a sieve until smooth.

....

PEACH PURÉE

There is nothing nicer than a ripe, juicy peach and it makes a delicious purée. Nectarines, plums and apricots are suitable alternatives. It's wise to make a larger quantity, especially if the fruit is in season, and freeze in portions for later use.

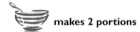 **makes 2 portions**

INGREDIENTS

1 ripe peach
2 tbsp water

1 Quarter the peach, removing the central stone then put it in a pan with the water. Bring to the boil then simmer the fruit for 8–10 minutes.

2 Remove the peach from the cooking water and when cool enough to handle, peel off the skin.

3 Transfer the peach to a blender and purée until smooth, adding a little boiled water, if necessary.

STORAGE TIP
Suitable for freezing

CARROT PURÉE

The wonderful colour and natural sweetness of carrot makes it a popular first food.

1 Scrape or peel the carrot then cut into bite-sized pieces. Put the carrot in a saucepan with the water. Bring to the boil and cook for 10 minutes until tender.

2 Put the carrot in a blender with a little of the cooking water and blend until a smooth purée.

VARIATION
When your baby is familiar with carrot, try puréeing it with cooked potato, butternut squash or pumpkin.

STORAGE TIP
Suitable for freezing

makes 2–3 portions

INGREDIENTS
1 carrot
2 tbsp water

AVOCADO PURÉE

Avocadoes are rich in nutrients and beneficial oils; they also make a perfect quick meal as they do not require cooking. Make sure you use a ripe avocado and prepare it just before serving as it discolours soon after cutting. You could leave out the yogurt, if preferred.

 **makes 1 portion**

INGREDIENTS

½ small avocado
2 tsp plain yogurt
(optional)

1 Cut the avocado in half lengthways and remove the stone. Scoop out the flesh into a bowl using a teaspoon.

2 Mash the avocado with a fork until smooth and creamy. Mix in the yogurt and stir thoroughly until combined. Serve immediately.

STORAGE TIP

Not suitable for freezing. Squeeze fresh lemon juice over the remaining half of avocado to prevent it discolouring. Keep the avocado in the fridge for use the following day.

SWEET POTATO PURÉE

Sweet potato makes a nutritious purée and a useful base for other mixed purées. The orange-fleshed ones are richer in vitamin C and beta carotene than those with a white flesh. Blend with breast or formula milk for a creamy textured purée.

 **makes 4–6 portions**

INGREDIENTS

1 small, orange-fleshed
sweet potato

1 Peel the sweet potato and cut into bite-sized chunks. Cover with water and bring to the boil and cook for 10–15 minutes until tender.

2 Drain the potatoes and transfer to a blender with a little breast or formula milk to make a smooth, creamy purée.

VARIATION

Yams and potatoes can also be prepared in the same way. When your baby is familiar with single-ingredient purées, you could combine these with a little grated cheese, cooked poultry, meat, fish, pulses or other vegetables.

MIXED PURÉES

Once your baby is familiar with a selection of single-ingredient purées, increase the range of flavours by combining different foods together. You also could increase the texture from thin, runny ones to more coarsely textured purées or even mashed or minced foods.

PEA & COURGETTE PURÉE

Courgettes have a light, slightly watery texture and combine well with more fibre-rich peas.
This can be mixed with potato, too.

1 Trim and slice the courgette; there is no need to peel it. Steam or boil the courgette and peas for 3 minutes until tender.

2 Mash until a coarse purée or transfer to a blender and purée until smooth, adding a little of the cooking water, if necessary.

VARIATION

Instead of the courgette, use 3 small florets of broccoli. Steam for 5 minutes before adding the peas and cook for a further 3 minutes until tender. Mash until a coarse purée or transfer to a blender and purée until smooth, adding a little of the cooking water, if necessary.

makes 2–4 portions

INGREDIENTS

1 courgette
Small handful of frozen
petit pois

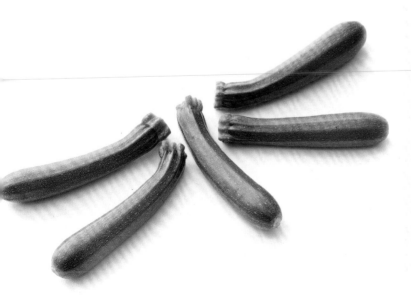

LEEK, POTATO & SWEETCORN PURÉE

This baby-friendly version of the classic corn chowder makes an excellent flavoursome purée.
Blend with breast or formula milk for a creamy texture.

 **makes 2–4 portions**

INGREDIENTS

1 potato
½ small leek
3 tbsp canned no sugar
  or salt sweetcorn

1 Peel the potato and cut into bite-sized chunks. Wash the leek, remove the tough outer layer then slice thinly.

2 Steam or boil the potatoes and leek for 12–15 minutes, adding the sweetcorn 3 minutes before the end of the cooking time. Cook until the vegetables are tender.

3 Transfer the vegetables to a blender and blend with a little breast or formula milk until puréed.

VARIATION

To increase the nutritional value or this mixed vegetable purée you could add a protein food such as grated cheese, cooked skinless chicken, white fish or a hard-boiled egg.

SQUASH, PARSNIP & APPLE PURÉE

Rich in vitamin C, this nourishing purée would also taste delicious as an accompaniment to roast pork. Purée or mash depending on desired consistency.

1 Wash, peel and dice the squash (removing any seeds) and the parsnip. Put the vegetables in a saucepan and cover with water. Bring to the boil then reduce the heat and simmer for 10 minutes.

2 While the vegetables are cooking, wash, peel, core and dice the apple and then add to the pan. Cook for another 5 minutes until everything is tender.

3 While the vegetables are cooking, wash, peel, core and dice the apple and then add to the pan. Cook for another 5 minutes until everything is tender.

STORAGE TIP
Suitable for freezing

makes 4–6 portions

INGREDIENTS

75g butternut squash
1 small parsnip
1 dessert apple

OAT & VEGETABLE PURÉE

Oats give extra substance to this vegetable purée.

1 Put the oats in a small saucepan and cover with water and bring to the boil. Reduce the heat and simmer, covered, for 4–5 minutes until soft and creamy. Stir the oats occasionally to prevent them sticking to the bottom of the pan.

2 While the oats are cooking, steam the leeks for 10 minutes until tender. Drain any excess water from the oats, if necessary, and add the leeks, tomato and sweetcorn to the pan with 2 tablespoons milk (breast, formula or cow's).

3 Add the butter to the pan and stir until heated through. Purée or mash depending on the desired consistency.

VARIATION
Try adding two tablespoons cooked and minced chicken or beef.

makes 4–6 portions

INGREDIENTS

2 tbsp rolled porridge oats
1 small leek, finely chopped
2 tbsp canned no-sugar or no-salt sweetcorn
1 tomato, skinned, seeded and chopped
small knob of unsalted butter or margarine

VEGETABLE & PASTA STEW

This is a nutritious combination of vegetables, pasta and beans, which provides a good range of vitamins and minerals.

 makes 4–6 portions

INGREDIENTS

- 1 tbsp olive oil
- 1 small onion
- 1 small carrot, scrubbed and finely diced
- ½ tsp dried oregano
- 300ml water
- 5 tbsp passata
- 50g small soup pasta
- 4 tbsp canned no-salt, no-sugar flageolet beans, drained and rinsed
- 25g baby spinach, finely chopped
- 2 tbsp freshly grated Parmesan cheese

1 Heat the olive oil in a medium-sized saucepan. Add the onion and carrot and cook, stirring, for 10 minutes until softened.

2 Add the oregano, water and passata. Bring to the boil then reduce the heat and simmer, covered, for 10 minutes.

3 Next, stir in the pasta and beans, return the soup to the boil and simmer until the pasta is tender, stirring occasionally. Add the spinach and cook for a further 2 minutes.

4 Stir in the Parmesan and purée, mash or chop depending on the desired consistency – you may need to add a little more boiled water if puréeing.

VARIATION

Instead of the pasta and beans, add 20g red split lentils in step 2 and cook for 20 minutes, adding more water if necessary. When the lentils are tender, stir in the spinach and cook according to the recipe.

CHICKEN WITH TOMATO RICE

This makes a satisfying and tasty addition to your baby's diet. You could try a combination of white and brown rice to increase nutrient levels.

1 Preheat the grill to medium-high and line the grill pan with foil. Put the chicken in the grill pan and brush with oil. Grill for 6–8 minutes each side until cooked through and there is no trace of pink.

2 While the chicken is cooking, put the rice and chopped tomatoes in a saucepan with the water. Bring to the boil and add the oregano, carrot and beans.

3 Reduce the heat, cover, and simmer for 15–20 minutes, or until the water has been absorbed and the vegetables are tender.

4 Finely chop the chicken and mix into the rice then purée or mince until the desired consistency – you may need to add a little extra boiled water.

VARIATION
In place of the chicken, grill a fillet of white fish for 10–15 minutes depending on the thickness. Remove the skin and any bones then flake the fish and stir into the rice.

STORAGE TIP
Suitable for freezing. If freezing the rice make sure it is completely defrosted before reheating. Heat through thoroughly to avoid any risk of food contamination.

makes 6–8 portions

INGREDIENTS

125g skinless, boneless chicken breast, cut into strips
olive oil, for brushing
75g white rice
6 tbsp canned chopped tomatoes
175ml water
½ tsp dried oregano
1 small carrot, scrubbed and finely diced
3 fine green beans, thinly sliced

BEAN & VEGETABLE MASH

This is a nutritious combination of vegetables, pasta and beans, which provides a good range of vitamins and minerals.

makes 4 portions

INGREDIENTS

1 potato, peeled
75g swede, beetroot, parsnip or celeriac, peeled
1 tsp olive oil
15g unsalted butter
4 tbsp no-salt, no-sugar baked beans
2 tbsp grated Cheddar

1 Cut the potato and swede, or root vegetable of choice, into bite-sized pieces and put in a saucepan. Cover with water and bring to the boil.

2 Reduce the heat and simmer for 15–20 minutes until tender. Drain and purée or mash the vegetables with the olive oil and butter.

3 Heat the beans gently then mash. Stir the beans into the root vegetable mash with the Cheddar.

VARIATION
Replace the cheese with the yolk of one hard-boiled egg. Peel the egg, discard the white then mash the yolk into the beans and vegetables.

STORAGE TIP
Suitable for freezing.

DESSERTS

Even small babies have a natural "sweet tooth," which can be satisfied with a fruit-based pudding. Since the fruit is mixed with yogurt, fromage frais or served iced, the cool temperature and smooth texture can be soothing for babies cutting their first teeth.

DRIED APRICOT PURÉE

Dried apricots are a good source of iron, a vital mineral especially since a baby's stores begin to diminish from around six months of age. Like other dried fruit, apricots are high in fibre so it's important that they are given in small amounts. Here, the apricots are mixed with natural yogurt to give a creamy purée.

1 Wash the apricots and cut them into small pieces. Put the apricots in a saucepan, cover with water and bring to the boil then reduce the heat and simmer for 20 minutes until very soft.

2 Transfer to a blender and blend until puréed, adding a little of the cooking water, if necessary. Leave to cool slightly then mix with the yogurt.

INGREDIENT TIP
Sulphur is commonly used to preserve dried fruit but is best avoided by those susceptible to asthma as it is known to exacerbate symptoms. Unsulphured apricots are dark brown in colour and have a rich, almost toffee-like flavour.

makes 5–8 portions

INGREDIENTS

10 unsulphured ready-to-eat dried apricots
3 tbsp natural yogurt

ORCHARD FRUIT YOGURT

It is worth making a larger portion of this stewed fruit for later use. Freeze the fruit mixture then defrost before mixing with the yogurt.

 makes 2–4 portions

INGREDIENTS

2 plums
1 dessert apple
2 tbsp water
4-6 tbsp natural yogurt
1 plain biscuit (optional)

1 Halve the plums and remove the stone. Peel, core and chop the apple into bite-sized pieces. Put the fruit in a saucepan and add the water.

2 Bring to the boil then reduce the heat and simmer for 5–8 minutes until tender. Remove the plum skins then purée the fruit in a blender or pass through a sieve.

3 Crush the biscuit, if using. Mix together the fruit and yogurt and sprinkle over the crushed biscuit, if using, before serving.

STORAGE TIP
Cooked fruit is suitable for freezing

BANANA YOGURT CUSTARD

This is the simplest of desserts and would also make a quick breakfast or snack. Make sure the banana is ripe as it will be easier for your baby to digest.

 makes 2–4 portions

INGREDIENTS

1 small banana, peeled
2 tbsp Greek yogurt
3 tbsp ready-made
   custard

Mash the banana until fairly smooth. Combine the banana, yogurt and custard then serve.

VARIATION
Replace the banana with 150g strawberries, hulled.

STORAGE TIP
Suitable for freezing

FRUIT FOOL

Not only is fresh mango packed with vitamin C, it is also delicious puréed. Combine with fromage frais and you have a quick fruit fool that can be served as a breakfast, dessert or snack.

1 | Peel the mango and cut away the flesh from the stone. Purée the fruit or pass through a sieve.

2 | Mix together the mango purée and fromage frais before serving.

makes 2–4 portions

INGREDIENTS

½ ripe mango
5 tbsp fromage frais

STORAGE TIP
Suitable for freezing

QUICK BANANA ICE CREAM

This speedy ice cream is perfect for soothing sore gums if your baby is teething.

1 | Peel the banana and wrap in cling film. Freeze until solid – about 3 hours.

2 | Remove the banana from the freezer and take off the cling film. Leave to soften slightly then mash with a fork.

makes 2 portions

INGREDIENTS

1 banana

STORAGE TIP
Suitable for freezing

BANANA & STRAWBERRY SMOOTHIE

It can sometimes be difficult to get children to eat breakfast, yet a smoothie served in a brightly coloured cup may be just the thing to renew interest. It is full of vital nutrients and provides much needed energy for the morning ahead. The fruit provide vitamin C and magnesium, while the milk and yogurt contain calcium, all essential for healthy skin, bones and teeth.

 1–2 child-size servings

 toast and a boiled egg for a nutritionally complete breakfast

INGREDIENTS

1 small banana, sliced
3 strawberries, hulled and halved if large
2 tbsp thick natural bio yogurt
4 tbsp milk (breast, formula, cow's or alternative)

Put all the ingredients in a blender and whiz until thick, smooth and creamy then pour the smoothie into cups or glasses, adding more milk, if necessary. (Straw optional.)

SERVING TIP

You could freeze the smoothie in a lidded pot to make a simple yogurt ice or alternatively, omit the milk and serve as a natural fruit yogurt.

STORAGE TIP

Smoothies don't generally keep longer than a day. Store any surplus smoothie in an airtight container in the fridge. Add a squeeze of lemon juice to help prevent the banana discolouring.

6 months

DATE & VANILLA BREAKFAST YOGURT

This thick and creamy fruit yogurt is a nourishing and energy-boosting blend of protein and slow-release carbohydrates, making it an excellent start to the day.

1 Put the dates and 150ml of water in a medium-sized saucepan. Bring to the boil then reduce the heat. Put a lid on and simmer for 10 minutes until the dates are soft. Leave to cool.

2 Put the dates and any remaining water, yogurt, vanilla extract and milk in a blender. Whiz until smooth and creamy. Spoon into a bowl.

SERVING TIP
You could freeze the yogurt in a lidded pot to make a simple yogurt ice or alternatively add extra milk (breast, formula, cow's or alternative) to make a nutritious smoothie.

STORAGE TIP
Store any surplus in an airtight container in the fridge for up to three days.

2 child-size servings

fingers of toasted fruit bread for dipping in

INGREDIENTS
60g dried, ready-to-eat, stoned
   dates, roughly chopped
60ml thick natural bio yogurt
½ tsp vanilla extract
4 tbsp milk (breast, formula,
   cow's or alternative)

6 months

APRICOT & PRUNE FRUIT SPREAD

A healthier alternative to commercial jams, this contains considerably more fruit and less sugar, and is an excellent source of vitamins and minerals, especially iron.

 makes 350g

 spread thinly on plain or toasted bread, muffins or crumpets

INGREDIENTS

115g ready-to-eat dried unsulphured apricots, roughly chopped
115g ready-to-eat dried prunes, roughly chopped
500ml water

1 Put the apricots and prunes in a non-metallic saucepan. Cover with 425 ml water and bring to the boil. Reduce the heat, cover, and simmer for 45 minutes until the fruit is very soft, swollen and almost caramelised.

2 Transfer the cooked fruit to a blender or food processor and blend with the remaining water to make a thick purée. Spoon the fruit spread into an airtight jar or container and store in the refrigerator for up to a week.

6+ months

THREE-NUT BUTTER

This home-made butter contains no additives or sugar unlike many commercial varieties.

 8 child-size servings

 spread thinly on toast, fingers of pitta bread or crumpets

INGREDIENTS

25g almonds, shelled
25g cashew nuts
25g peanuts, shelled
3-4 tablespoons sunflower oil

1 Toast the nuts in a dry frying pan for 2–5 minutes. Rub the nuts in a clean tea towel to remove the papery brown covering, if necessary.

2 Transfer the nuts to a food processor or blender and process until finely ground.

3 Pour the oil into the blender or food processor and blend to a coarse paste. Store in an airtight jar or container in the refrigerator for up to a week.

 6 months

Note Contains nuts: avoid serving to babies if there is a history of nut allergy, asthma, hay fever or eczema within the immediate family. Please consult your doctor.

GOLDEN CRUNCH

It is important to include a good range of essential fatty acids in a child's diet and the nuts and seeds in this granola provide a nourishing mix of both omega-3 and omega-6 fatty acids. If serving to babies under a year, finely grind the cereal and cook and purée the apricots.

1 Preheat the oven to 140°C (275°F). Put the oats, almonds, pecans and seeds in a large bowl.

2 Heat the oil and maple syrup in a saucepan over a medium heat, stirring until melted and mixed together. Stir into the oats, nuts and seeds then mix well until they are thoroughly coated.

3 Spoon onto two baking sheets in an even layer and bake in the preheated oven for 25 minutes, turning halfway, until golden and slightly crisp. (The mixture will become crisper as it cools.)

4 Return the cereal to a bowl and mix in the chopped apricots. Leave to cool then transfer to an airtight container.

VARIATION

For a special breakfast treat, place two to three slices of banana in the bottom of a tall glass. Top with 1 tbsp of live, natural bio yogurt, followed by 1 tsp Golden Crunch (without the dried apricots). Top with another tbsp of the yoghurt and decorate with two to three more slices of banana. Makes 1 child-size serving.

STORAGE TIP

Store Golden Crunch in an airtight jar or container for up to three weeks.

12 child-size servings

pour on milk (breast, formula, cow's or alternative); top with fresh fruit such as chopped or puréed strawberries, mashed banana or stewed pear or apple

INGREDIENTS

100g whole porridge oats
40g flaked almonds
30g pecan halves, roughly broken
25g sesame seeds
25g sunflower seeds
1½ tbsp sunflower oil
3 tbsp maple syrup
50g ready-to-eat unsulphured dried apricots, finely chopped

8 months

Note Contains nuts (and seeds); avoid serving to babies if there is a history of nut allergy, asthma, hay fever or eczema within the immediate family. Please consult your doctor.

SEEDY BANANA BREAKFAST

This simple breakfast provides plenty of essential vitamins and minerals. Live natural bio yogurt has a thick, smooth consistency and contains beneficial bacteria which restores equilibrium in the gut.

 1–2 child-size servings

 with toast

INGREDIENTS

1 tbsp mixed seeds such as sunflower, pumpkin and sesame

1 small banana, mashed

6 tbsp live natural bio yogurt

2 tsp maple syrup (optional)

1 Lightly toast the seeds in a dry frying pan until just golden, tossing frequently. Transfer them to a grinder and process until finely ground.

2 Mix together the banana and yogurt, then stir in the seeds. Drizzle each serving with the maple syrup, if using.

SERVING TIP

You could make a larger quantity of the ground seed mixture then stir a spoonful into sauces, soups, burgers and vegetarian roasts to enhance their nutritional value.

Note This breakfast contains seeds; avoid serving to babies if there is a history of nut allergy, asthma, hay fever or eczema within the immediate family. Please consult your doctor

8+ months

PORRIDGE WITH APRICOT PURÉE

Porridge is an excellent breakfast for young children – not only does it taste good, but research has shown that children who eat a carbohydrate-based breakfast, such as porridge, have improved concentration and so perform better at school.

1 To make the apricot purée, place the apricots in a saucepan and cover with the water. Bring to the boil, cover the pan, then reduce the heat and simmer for 30 minutes until the apricots are very tender. Place the apricots, along with any water left in the pan, in a blender or food processor and purée until smooth, adding more water if necessary.

2 To make the porridge, put the oats into a saucepan. Add the milk and bring to the boil, stirring occasionally. Reduce the heat and simmer, stirring frequently, for 6 minutes until smooth and creamy.

3 Pour the porridge into a bowl and stir in a large spoonful of the apricot purée.

VARIATION

Dried dates, prunes and figs make delicious fruit purées and are an excellent source of iron. Use the same method as for the apricot purée and top with a sprinkling of lightly roasted chopped flaked almonds for a delicious, nutritious breakfast if there is no history of nut allergy within the family.

You could use half-milk, half-water to make the porridge. Instead of the apricot purée, try mashed banana or stewed pear or apple.

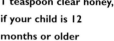

**1–4 child-size servings
(purée serves 4–6)**

**1 teaspoon clear honey,
if your child is 12
months or older**

INGREDIENTS

Apricot purée
115g ready-to-eat dried
    apricots
300ml water

Porridge
55g porridge oats
125ml milk (breast, formula,
    cow's or alternative) or half
    milk, half water

6 months

BREAKFAST OMELETTE

Children love this complete breakfast in a pan, which is rather similar to an Spanish omelette. This makes a substantial weekend breakfast-cum-brunch or also makes a perfect supper dish. If serving to young infants, make sure they are ready to eat finger foods or you could try mashing the omelette with baked beans.

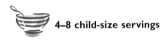 **4–8 child-size servings**

 **baked beans and toast**

INGREDIENTS

3 good quality sausages (or vegetarian alternative)
4 cooked medium-size potatoes, cooled and cut into bite-sized chunks
6 cherry tomatoes, halved
4 eggs, beaten
sunflower oil, for frying

1 Preheat the grill to medium-high. Arrange the sausages on a foil-lined grill pan then grill until cooked through and golden. Leave to cool slightly, then slice into small chunks.

2 Meanwhile, heat a little oil in a medium-sized heavy-based frying pan with an ovenproof handle. Cook the potatoes until lightly golden all over, then add the tomatoes and cook for a further 2 minutes.

3 Arrange the sausages in the pan so there is an even distribution of potatoes, tomatoes and sausages.

4 Add a little more oil to the pan if it seems dry. Pour the beaten eggs over the ingredients in the pan. Cook for 3 minutes without stirring or disturbing the omelette.

5 Place under the preheated grill for an additional 3 minutes until the top is just cooked. Serve mashed with beans or cut into wedges and serve with toast.

8 months

TOMATO & EGG SCRAMBLE

This simple breakfast or light lunch is a good source of iron and B vitamins. Make sure the eggs are well cooked and there is no sign of runniness before serving. If you haven't progressed to finger foods with your baby, leave out the bagel until you feel he or she is at the right stage.

1 Heat the butter in a heavy-based medium-sized saucepan. Add the tomatoes and cook for 2 minutes until softened, stirring occasionally.

2 Lightly beat the egg with the milk. Pour the mixture into the pan and using a wooden spoon, stir constantly to ensure the egg doesn't stick to the bottom of the pan. Continue to cook the egg, stirring, until it is cooked and not runny – this should take about 4 minutes.

3 Meanwhile, toast and butter the bagel and cut into wedges. Serve with the scrambled egg.

PREPARATION TIP

For babies, you may prefer to peel the tomato beforehand. Make a cross-shaped slit in the top of the tomato and place it in boiled water for one minute to loosen the skin. Scoop out the tomato with a slotted spoon and peel off the skin, if it refuses to peel put the tomato back in the water. When skinned, cut the tomato into quarters, scoop out the seeds and finely chop.

1 child-size serving

toasted bagel along with a glass of very diluted fresh orange juice to encourage the absorption of iron from the eggs

INGREDIENTS

15g unsalted butter, plus extra to serve
1 medium tomato, seeded and diced
2 small free-range eggs
1 tbsp milk (breast, formula, cow's or alternative)
½ bagel

6 months

EGGY BREAD

Bread dipped in an egg-and-milk mixture makes great finger food and, for added appeal, cut the bread into fun shapes – diamonds, hearts or flowers – before dipping into the egg.

 **2 child-size servings**

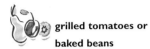 **grilled tomatoes or baked beans**

INGREDIENTS

1-2 slices of wholemeal or
  white bread
1 egg, beaten
1 tbsp milk (breast, formula,
  cow's or alternative)
Butter, for frying

1. Cut the bread into the desired shapes with pastry cutters or leave as a slice if preferred. Whisk together the egg and milk in a wide, shallow bowl and dip the bread shapes into the mixture.

2. Heat some butter in a heavy-based frying pan, place the bread in the pan and cook, turning once, until the egg has set and is well cooked and golden. Serve immediately.

VARIATION

For a sweet version, prepare and cook as above but sprinkle over a little caster sugar and ground cinnamon before serving.

7 months

HAM & EGG CUPS

Eggs make a nutritious start to the day, providing much needed protein, vitamins D and B and zinc but for young children must be thoroughly cooked; these cups make great finger food.

 4 child-size servings

toast and grilled, skinned tomatoes

INGREDIENTS

olive oil, for greasing
4 slices lean ham
4 free-range eggs

1. Preheat the oven to 200°C (400°F). Lightly grease four holes of a deep muffin tin and arrange a slice of ham in each one, overlapping the sides to make it fit and form a "cup" shape.

2. Trim the top of the ham to make it even but make sure it is still slightly above the top of the tin.

3. Crack an egg into each ham-lined muffin hole then bake for 10 minutes, or until both the whites and yolks are firm and set.

4. Remove from the oven and leave to cool slightly before removing the pies from the tin.

STORAGE TIP
The ham pies will keep in the fridge for up to two days.

8 months

EGG CUPS

Baby brioche are great for filling with all manner of sweet and savoury goodies. Scrambled egg makes a great filling and is also a good source of iron and protein. If your baby hasn't progressed to finger foods, leave out the brioche until you feel he or she is ready.

1 Preheat the oven to 140°C (275°F). Wrap the brioche in foil and warm in the oven.

2 Meanwhile, heat the butter in a heavy-based saucepan. When it has melted, add the eggs. Using a wooden spoon, stir constantly, to to ensure the egg doesn't stick to the bottom of the pan. Continue to cook the egg, stirring, until the eggs are scrambled thoroughly and not runny – this should take about 4 minutes.

3 Slice off the top of each brioche and scoop out the centre. Spoon the scrambled egg into the brioche cups and sprinkle with the chives, if using. Replace the lids of the brioches before serving or alternatively, cut into fingers.

1–2 child-size servings

to serve as finger food, cut the brioche into strips and omit chives

INGREDIENTS

1-2 small brioche buns
2 eggs, beaten
25g unsalted butter
Few snipped chives, to garnish
  (optional)

7
months

MINI BANANA PANCAKES

These pancakes make an energizing breakfast and would also make a suitable snack or dessert.
Bananas are a good source of potassium, which plays a key role in nerve cell function.

 about 10 pancakes
1 pancake will serve an
eight month old

 fresh fruit and a drizzle of maple syrup

INGREDIENTS

100g self-raising flour
1 tbsp caster sugar
½ tsp bicarbonate of soda
1 egg, lightly beaten
100ml milk
2 tbsp thick natural yogurt
1 banana, mashed
Sunflower oil, for frying

1 Sift the flour, sugar, and bicarbonate of soda into a mixing bowl. Make a well in the centre of the flour mixture.

2 Beat the eggs with the milk in a jug and gradually pour into the bowl, whisking continuously to avoid any lumps. Add the yogurt and stir to make a smooth and creamy batter. Set the batter aside for 20 minutes then stir in the banana.

3 Lightly oil a large heavy-based frying pan and wipe with a folded sheet of kitchen towel to remove any excess. Heat the pan until hot then place two tablespoons of batter per pancake – you will probably be able to cook three pancakes at a time – in the pan.

4 Cook each pancake for 2–3 minutes, or until the base is light golden then turn over and cook for a further minute. Place the pancakes on a plate and cover with foil to keep them warm while you make the remaining pancakes.

5 To serve as finger food, cut into strips. Alternatively, top with banana slices or fruit of choice and maple syrup.

STORAGE TIP
Pancakes freeze well so you could make larger quantities and keep some for future use: defrost then wrap in foil and warm in the oven.

8 months

POTATO CAKES WITH BEANS

A great way of using up leftover mashed potato, these savoury mini pancakes can be served on their own or alongside grilled tomatoes, or good quality sausages or bacon. They also make ideal finger food.

1 Beat together the mashed potato and milk in a bowl to make a coarse potato purée.

4 cakes
I cake will serve an eight month old
grilled tomatoes, sausages or bacon

2 Put the flour in a separate bowl, make a well in the centre and add the beaten egg, then gradually add the potato purée. Whisk to make a smooth, creamy, fairly thick batter.

3 Heat a little oil in a large non-stick frying pan. Ladle one-quarter of the batter into the pan for each pancake and cook for 2 minutes on each side until golden. You may have to make the pancakes in batches and if so, keep the finished ones warm while you cook the remaining potato cakes.

INGREDIENTS

60g cold mashed potato
90ml milk (breast, formula, cow's or alternative)
75g self-raising flour
I small egg, beaten
sunflower oil, for frying
150-200g tin no-salt or sugar baked beans

4 Warm the baked beans in a pan and serve with the potato cakes, which can be cut into fingers if preferred.

STORAGE TIP
The potato cakes freeze well and will keep for up to three months in a freezer. Make up to step 3, allow to cool, then freeze in between sheets of greaseproof paper to prevent them sticking together. Defrost and warm in the oven before serving.

8 months

SIMPLE HUMOUS

This delicious alternative to the shop-bought dips is made with calcium-rich sesame seed paste, tahini, and also contains valuable iron and B vitamins provided by the chickpeas. You could stir a spoonful in soups and stews as well as serving it as a dip.

 about 7 child-size servings

 finger foods such as breadsticks, rice cakes, steamed vegetable sticks

INGREDIENTS

200g can chickpeas (about
    120g drained weight),
    drained and rinsed
Juice of ½ lemon
½ clove garlic, crushed
1 tbsp tahini (sesame seed
    paste)
2 tbsp extra-virgin olive oil
2 tbsp water

1 Put the chickpeas in a food processor or blender with the lemon juice, garlic, tahini, olive oil and water.

2 Process until puréed – you will have to stir the humous occasionally during blending to keep the mixture moving. Add extra water if the humous is too thick.

3 Place one to two tablespoons in a small bowl and serve with finger foods. Spoon the remainder into an airtight container.

STORAGE TIP

Simple Humous will keep up to one week stored in the fridge in an airtight container.

7-8 months

CREAMY GUACAMOLE

Avocados provide useful amounts of protein, carbohydrate and monounsaturated fat. They also contain the highest concentration of vitamin E of any fruit. The mayonnaise gives this guacamole a creamy consistency, which is more appealing to children and you could leave out the garlic, if preferred.

Put the avocado flesh into a bowl and mash with a fork until smooth. Add the mayonnaise, tomato, garlic, if using, and lemon juice then mix well until combined.

STORAGE TIP
Creamy Guacamole can be kept in the fridge in an airtight container for up to two days

about 2–4 child-size servings

finger foods such as breadsticks, rice cakes, steamed vegetable sticks

INGREDIENTS
I small ripe avocado, stoned and flesh scooped out
I tsp mayonnaise
I small tomato, peeled, deseeded and finely chopped
½ clove garlic, crushed (optional)
I tsp lemon juice

7-8 months

TOMATO & BEAN DIP

This creamy dip makes a quick, nutritious snack. It is delicious spread on different breads or used as a dip with finger foods.

 about 10 child-size servings

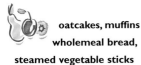 **oatcakes, muffins wholemeal bread, steamed vegetable sticks**

INGREDIENTS

3 vine-ripened tomatoes, quartered and seeded

3 cloves garlic, left whole in their skin

2 tbsp extra-virgin olive oil

200g can cannellini beans, drained and rinsed

2 tbsp fresh lemon juice

1 Preheat the oven to 200°C (400°F). Place the tomatoes and garlic with half of the olive oil in a roasting pan. Roast for 15 minutes until the garlic is soft and the tomatoes tender.

2 Peel the garlic and tomatoes and place in a food processor or blender with the rest of the oil, beans and lemon juice. Purée the bean mixture until smooth then store in the refrigerator in an airtight container.

STORAGE TIP

The Tomato & Bean Dip will keep in an airtight container in the fridge for up to one week.

7-8 months

Fresh vegetables, lightly steamed for babies without many teeth, and breadsticks make ideal finger food on their own as well as baby "cruditées" for eating with a variety of dips.

AUBERGINE PURÉE

Aubergines make a nutritious (rich in B vitamins and C) and surprisingly creamy dip.

1 Preheat the oven to 200°C (400°F). Put the aubergine in an oiled roasting tin. Roast for about 30 to 35 minutes, or until the flesh is very soft when pressed with a finger.

2 Leave to cool slightly then cut the aubergine in half lengthways and scoop out the flesh with a spoon; discard the skin.

3 Put the cooked aubergine into a food processor or blender with the olive oil, garlic, spices, lemon juice and tahini. Blend to make a smooth and creamy dip.

STORAGE TIP
The Aubergine Dip will keep in an airtight container in the fridge for up to one week.

8-9
months

about 4 child-size servings

finger foods such as breadsticks, rice cakes, steamed vegetables sticks

INGREDIENTS

I small aubergine
I tbsp olive oil, plus extra for greasing
I clove garlic, chopped
½ tsp ground cumin
½ tsp ground coriander
Juice of ½ lemon
I tbsp tahini (sesame seed paste)

SARDINES ON TOAST FINGERS

Fresh sardines are incredibly bony so tend not to be popular with children. However, the canned variety make a useful, nutritious alternative and still provide beneficial brain oils. Furthermore, the sardines are mixed with fresh tomato and pesto to dilute any fishiness.

 1 child-size portion

 on their own

INGREDIENTS

1 slice wholemeal bread
2 boned sardines in tomato
  sauce
1 heaped tsp red pesto
1 cherry tomato, seeded and
  chopped

1 Preheat the grill to medium-high. Line a grill pan with foil. Mash the sardines and mix with the pesto and tomato.

2 Toast one side of the bread, then turn over and lightly toast the other side. Spoon the sardine mixture on top and grill for 3 minutes until heated through.

3 Leave to cool slightly then cut into fingers.

VARIATION

Use other canned fish like mackerel, pilchards or kippers instead of the sardines. All are rich in omega-3 fatty acids.

Note Pesto contains pinenuts, which are not recommended for babies with a family history of nut allergy.

8 months

EGG TOASTS

This makes a fun snack: cut out a round in the centre of a slice of bread and replace it with an egg. Add vegetables if serving for lunch.

 about 1 child-size serving

 grilled tomatoes or baked beans

INGREDIENTS

1 slice wholemeal bread
1 egg
butter, for spreading

1 Preheat the grill to high. Stamp out a circle, about 5cm in diameter, in the centre of the slice of bread using a pastry cutter.

2 Line the grill pan with foil. Toast one side of the bread. Turn the bread over, spread the top with butter and break the egg into the hole in the centre. Grill for about 5 minutes until both the white and yolk are set.

8 months

CINNAMON FRENCH TOAST

This makes a delicious finger food or a brunch dish and also can be served for dessert. The French toast comes with sliced bananas but you could serve it with any favourite fresh fruit such as strawberries or sliced pear to add a nutritional boost.

1 Use a fork to mix together the egg, milk and cinnamon in a shallow dish. Melt the butter in a non-stick frying pan and swirl it around to coat the base evenly.

2 Dip both sides of the brioche slice in the egg mixture then allow any excess to drip off.

3 Cook for about 2 minutes each side or until the egg is set and light golden.

1 child-size serving

sliced or mashed banana

INGREDIENTS

1 egg, lightly beaten
1 tbsp semi-skimmed milk
Pinch of ground cinnamon
Small knob of butter
1 slice bread, brioche or panettone or 1 small fruit bun

8 months

BREADSTICKS

These breadsticks make an energy-boosting snacks eaten on their own or dipped into humous or similar alternative. Store in an airtight container for a couple of days or freeze for future use.

 25 sticks

 on their own or with dip

INGREDIENTS

2 tsp olive oil
250g strong white flour, plus extra for dusting
3g instant dried yeast
½ tsp salt (optional)
150ml lukewarm water
1 small egg, beaten

1 In a large bowl, mix together the flour with the yeast and salt, if using. Add the water and the oil, mixing initially with a wooden spoon and then your hands to make a soft, slightly sticky dough, adding more water or flour if the mixture seems too dry or wet.

2 Dust a work surface with flour and knead the dough for 10 minutes – push the dough flat with the palm of your hand then fold the far edge towards you, giving it a half turn, then repeat the process. Place the dough in a clean bowl, cover with a tea towel and leave it to rest somewhere warm and out of a draught for 10 minutes.

3 Preheat the oven to 220°C (425°F). Roll out the dough into a thin rectangle, halve the dough horizontally and cut into 1-cm wide strips. Roll each piece of dough into a sausage-shape using both hands and place on a lightly floured baking sheet. You will need 2 baking sheets as this dough makes about 25 breadsticks. Cover each sheet with a clean tea towel and set aside for 15 minutes, or until risen.

4 Mix together the beaten egg and milk and brush the mixture lightly over each breadstick. Bake for 15 minutes until crisp and golden. Transfer to a wire rack to cool.

SEEDY BREADSTICKS

Lightly toast two tablespoons of sunflower seeds in a dry frying pan. Transfer to a food processor with one tablespoon of olive oil and grind to make a rough paste. Set aside to cool then mix into the dough mixture in step 1.

CHEESY BREADSTICKS

Roll out the dough into a thin rectangle as in step 3, then sprinkle 100g Gruyère cheese over the top. Fold the pastry in half and roll out again to seal the edges. Cut into long 1-cm strips, then cut each strip in half and gently twist. Place on lightly greased baking sheets, brush with the glaze and bake as above.

8 months

CHEESY PEOPLE

These mini "people-shaped" cheese scones make a fun snack.

1 Preheat the oven to 220°C (425°F) and lightly grease two baking sheets. Sift both types of flour and baking powder into a large bowl.

2 Rub in the butter with your fingertips until the mixture forms coarse breadcrumbs. Stir in the cheese and make a hollow in the middle. Pour in the egg and milk and mix initially with a wooden spoon and then with your hands to make a soft dough.

3 Turn out the dough on a lightly floured work surface and gently press into a round about 2.5cm thick. Stamp out the 12 "people" using small gingerbread people cutters. Place on the prepared baking sheets, brush the tops with milk, and bake for 12–15 minutes until risen and golden. Transfer to a wire rack to cool.

VARIATION

To make cheese scones, follow the instructions up to step 3 and after rolling out the dough, use a 5cm round cutter to stamp out 12 rounds. Brush with the egg and milk mixture and bake as above.

12 "people"

on their own

INGREDIENTS

120g plain flour
120g wholemeal flour
2 tsp baking powder
4 tbsp chilled butter, cubed
3 tbsp freshly grated
  Parmesan cheese
1 egg, beaten
100ml milk, plus extra for
  glazing

COUNTRY GARDEN SALAD

It is a good idea to introduce children to salads as early as possible. This is a great one to start with, since it contains a combination of fruit, vegetables and cheese. They also can eat it with their fingers!

 2 child-size servings

 boiled new potatoes or slice of bread with butter or spread

INGREDIENTS

Dressing
1 tbsp extra-virgin olive oil
1 tsp white wine vinegar
1 tsp mayonnaise

Salad
8 cherry tomatoes, halved
4 baby corn, blanched and
   sliced into rounds
8 white or black seedless
   grapes, halved
4 slices green pepper
2 slices Cheddar cheese

1 To make the dressing, whisk together the oil, vinegar and mayonnaise.

2 Place the tomatoes, corn and grapes and green pepper in a bowl. Spoon over the dressing and toss well.

3 Cut the cheese into small pieces and sprinkle over the top of the salad.

PREPARATION TIP
Encourage your child to eat salad by making it more interesting – the vegetables and cheese can be cut into leaves or flowers, or any shapes you can think of! Feel free to change the ingredients in this salad, depending on likes and dislikes. Carrots, red pepper, cucumber, watercress or even toasted nuts and seeds all make delicious additions.

 12 months

HALLOUMI & PITTA SALAD

This chunky salad is best eaten with the fingers if serving to young children. You could add cubes of Edam or Cheddar instead of the halloumi, if liked, but if sticking to the latter, give it a rinse first to remove any salty residue.

1 Preheat the grill to medium. Grill the pitta bread until light golden and slightly crisp; leave to cool. Meanwhile, mix together the ingredients for the dressing, if using.

2 Cut the cucumber lengthways into quarters then remove the seeds and cut into manageable chunks or sticks. Cut the pepper into manageable chunks or sticks.

3 Put the cucumber and pepper in a serving bowl then add the olives, if using. Pour the dressing over and toss until combined.

4 Heat a little oil in a frying pan and fry the halloumi until beginning to colour. Leave to cool to just warm and mix with the rest of the salad. Serve with the pitta bread fingers.

STORAGE TIP

If not serving this salad at one sitting, store the ingredients individually and keep for up to two days.

1–2 child-size servings

on its own

INGREDIENTS

Salad
1 small pitta bread, cut into fingers
2.5cm piece cucumber
¼ small red pepper
25g halloumi, rinsed, patted dry and cut into cubes
3 pitted black olives, halved (optional)

Dressing (optional)
1 tbsp extra-virgin olive oil, plus extra for frying
½ tsp white wine vinegar

12 months

HOME-MADE BAKED BEANS

Canned baked beans often contain excessive amounts of sugar and salt but by making your own you can control what ingredients you use. Beans are nutritious but also high in fibre and therefore should not be given to young babies in large quantities because they may find them difficult to digest.

 2–4 child-size servings

 toast or bread

INGREDIENTS

1 tbsp olive oil

200g can low-sugar and salt haricot beans, drained and rinsed

150ml passata (sieved tomatoes)

1–2 teaspoons Dijon mustard

1 tsp Worcestershire sauce

1 tsp maple syrup

1 tbsp tomato purée

1 Place all the ingredients in a heavy-based saucepan and mix together thoroughly. Bring to the boil, then reduce the heat and simmer 10 minutes.

2 Half-cover the pan and simmer for a further 10 minutes until the beans are tender and the sauce has reduced and thickened.

VARIATION
Serve the beans topped with grated Cheddar cheese.

STORAGE TIP
The baked beans can be kept in the fridge in an airtight container for up to two days.

BUBBLE & SQUEAK CAKES

Any leftover vegetables can be transformed into these delicious potato cakes – they are a perfect way to encourage children to eat cabbage! They can be mashed or cut into pieces for younger eaters.

1 Cook the potatoes in plenty of boiling salted water for 15 minutes, or until tender. Drain well and mash until smooth.

2 Meanwhile, steam the cabbage for 5 minutes, or until tender, then finely chop.

3 Combine the potatoes and cabbage with the mustard, spring onions (if using) and egg in a bowl. Mix well with a wooden spoon and leave to cool.

4 Shape the potato mixture into eight cakes using floured hands and dusting each cake in flour.

5 Heat enough oil to coat the bottom of a heavy-based frying pan. Fry the cakes in batches over a medium heat for 3–4 minutes on each side, until golden.

VARIATION
Peas, carrots, green beans and onion can be used instead of, or as well as, the cabbage. A handful of grated cheese mixed into the potato mash also tastes great.

8 cakes

I cake will serve an eight month old

grilled tomatoes, beans or a dollop of ketchup

INGREDIENTS

675g potatoes, diced
175g Savoy cabbage, finely
   shredded
I tbsp Dijon mustard
2 spring onions, finely
   chopped (optional)
I egg, beaten
Flour, for dusting
Vegetable oil, for frying

8 months

BAKED POTATOES

Wholesome, nutritious and easy to prepare, the inside of a baked potato is suitable for babies from six months. The skin can be served as finger food from eight months.

 makes 4

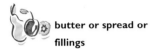 butter or spread or fillings

INGREDIENTS

4 x 120g baking potatoes, washed

Butter or polyunsaturated spread

1 Preheat the oven to 200°C (400°F). Prick the potatoes a few times with a fork or insert a skewer into the centre. Bake for one to one and a half hours until the skin is crisp and the inside is soft. Remove the skewer, if using, and cut the potatoes in half.

2 Top the potatoes with butter or spread or alternatively add one of the fillings suggested opposite.

8 months

PESTO & AVOCADO FILLING

INGREDIENTS

1 medium avocado, stoned
  and flesh scooped out
1 tbsp mayonnaise
1 tsp lemon juice
1 tbsp green pesto
Freshly grated Parmesan
  cheese (optional)

1 | Put the avocado flesh into a bowl and mash with a fork until smooth. Add the mayonnaise, lemon juice and pesto and mix until combined.

2 | Spoon the avocado mixture on top of baked potatoes and sprinkle with Parmesan cheese (if using). If serving to young babies, scoop out the potato and mash with the filling. The skin can be cut into strips and served as finger food if your baby has reached this stage.

Note Contains pinenuts, which are not recommended for babies with a history of nut allergy within the family.

HUMOUS & ROASTED RED PEPPER FILLING

INGREDIENTS

1 medium red pepper,
  deseeded and sliced
1 tbsp olive oil
4 tbsp humous

1 | While the potatoes are cooking, place the pepper on a baking tray and toss in the oil. Roast for 30–40 minutes, turning occasionally, until tender and the skin is slightly blackened in areas.

2 | Put the pepper in a plastic bag and leave for a few minutes; this makes it easier to peel. Remove the skin and cut the pepper in half. Scoop out the seeds then finely chop or purée the flesh.

3 | Combine the pepper with the humous and olive oil and spoon the mixture over the baked potatoes. If serving to young babies, scoop out the potato and mash with the filling. The skin can be cut into strips and served as finger food if your baby has reached this stage.

CREAM CHEESE & LEEK FILLING

INGREDIENTS

1 medium leek, finely chopped
1 tbsp olive oil
4 heaped tbsp cream cheese
1 tbsp finely chopped chives

Fry the leek in the olive oil for 5 minutes until softened. Remove from the heat and stir in the cream cheese with the chives. Spoon on top of the baked potatoes.

SESAME POTATO WEDGES

These potato wedges make great finger food. They are healthier than chips because they retain their nutritious skin and are baked in the oven, which keeps fat levels down. You also can use orange-fleshed sweet potatoes, which are rich in vitamin C and beta carotene.

 2–4 child-size servings

 low-sugar ketchup, humous or dip

INGREDIENTS

350g potatoes, scrubbed and
   cut into wedges
1 tbsp olive oil
1 tsp sesame seeds (optional)

1   Preheat the oven to 200°C (400°F).

2   Toss the potatoes in the oil and place on a baking tray. Bake for 25 minutes, then remove from the oven. Turn the potatoes, making sure they are thoroughly coated in the oil, and sprinkle with the sesame seeds, if using.

3   Return the potatoes to the oven for a further 15–20 minutes until tender and golden.

Note *This dish contains seeds – avoid serving to babies if there is a history of nut allergy, asthma, hay fever or eczema within the immediate family. Please consult your doctor.*

8-9 months

RICE & VEGETABLE FRITTERS

This recipe is perfect for using up any leftover rice and makes great finger food when cut up. Brown rice is used here because it is a good source of B vitamins and fibre, but white rice is also suitable.

1 Mix the rice with the spring onions, red pepper, garlic, egg, cream and flour.

2 Heat enough oil to coat the bottom of a heavy-based frying pan. Place two heaped dessertspoons of the rice mixture per fritter into the hot oil and flatten slightly with the back of a spoon. Cook in batches for 3 minutes on each side, until golden and drain on kitchen paper.

4–8 child-size servings

steamed green beans and broccoli

INGREDIENTS

85g long-grain brown rice, cooked and cooled
2 spring onions, sliced
½ red pepper, diced
1 clove garlic, crushed
1 small egg, beaten
2 tbsp double cream
2 tbsp plain flour
Sunflower oil, for frying

7-8 months

PEA SOUP

Soups are a perfect way of encouraging children to eat vegetables. You could also add less water to make a thicker soup or purée. When your baby is older – 12 months or more – you can make the soup with low-salt stock instead of water.

4 servings
(2 children, 2 adults)

bread sprinkled with
grated Cheddar cheese

INGREDIENTS

1 tbsp vegetable oil
1 leek, finely sliced
1 stick celery, finely chopped
225g potato, diced
1 litre water
280g frozen petit pois or
   garden peas

1 Heat the oil in a large, heavy-based saucepan. Add the leek and fry over a medium heat for 5 minutes or until softened. Add the celery and potato and cook for a further 5 minutes.

2 Pour the water over the vegetables and bring to the boil. Cover, reduce the heat and simmer the soup for 15 minutes. Add the peas and cook for a further 5 minutes or until the potato is tender.

3 Using a hand-blender or food processor, blend the soup until smooth. Reheat the soup, if necessary, before serving. For the adult servings, season to taste with salt and pepper.

STORING TIP

Soups freeze well and will keep for up to three months. You could freeze the Pea Soup in convenient child-size portions.

6 months

MISO NOODLE SOUP

This soup is very quick to make as it has a base of instant miso soup. Miso is made from fermented soya beans and is rich in minerals, particularly iron and calcium.

1 Steam the green beans and carrot until tender.

2 Meanwhile, cook the noodles in plenty of boiling water following the manufacturer's instructions. Add the spinach 2 minutes before the end of the cooking time. Drain the noodles and spinach and cut into manageable-sized pieces.

3 Make the miso soup, following the manufacturer's instructions. Place the noodles, carrots and beans in a serving bowl; chop them first if suitable for your baby. Pour the miso soup over the top. Stir in the soy sauce, if using.

4 Leave the soup to cool to the right temperature then serve garnished with the spring onion and sesame seeds (if using).

12 months

2 child-size servings

to make a more substantial soup, add minced cubes of marinated tofu or strips of cooked chicken.

INGREDIENTS

6 fine green beans, finely chopped
1 small carrot, finely chopped
1 sachet instant miso soup powder
50g egg or rice noodles
Handful of fresh baby spinach leaves, shredded
1 tsp reduced-salt soy sauce (optional)
1 spring onion, finely shredded and sesame seeds, to garnish (optional)

Note The soup contains seeds and soya, both of which have been linked to allergies. Avoid if there is any history of allergies in the family.

TOMATO & LENTIL SOUP

Tomato soup is a national favourite but shop-bought versions contain a surprising amount of fat and sugar. This nutritious homemade version features the added health benefit of lentils and doesn't take an age to make. With babies older than 12 months, you can make the soup with low-salt stock and add a dash of pepper.

4 servings
(2 children, 2 adults)

bread sprinkled with
grated Cheddar cheese

INGREDIENTS

50g split red lentils, rinsed
1 tbsp olive oil
1 onion, chopped
1 carrot, finely chopped
1 stick celery, finely chopped
500ml passata
500ml water
1 bay leaf
3 tbsp milk (optional)

1 Place the lentils in a saucepan, cover with water and bring to the boil. Reduce the heat and simmer, half-covered, for 15 minutes or until just tender. Remove any scum that rises to the surface using a spoon. Drain the lentils well and set aside.

2 Heat the oil in a large heavy-based saucepan. Add the onion, cover the pan and saute for 8 minutes until softened and transparent. Add the carrot and celery, cover, and cook for a further 3 minutes, stirring occasionally to prevent the vegetables sticking to the bottom of the pan.

3 Add the passata, water, lentils and bay leaf. Bring to the boil. Reduce the heat and simmer, half-covered, for 30 minutes until the lentils and vegetables are tender and the soup has thickened.

4 Carefully pour the soup into a blender or use a hand blender to purée the soup until smooth. Return to the pan and stir in the milk, if using. Reheat, if necessary, and serve.

STORAGE TIP
Tomato & Lentil Soup can be kept for up to three months in the freezer. Try freezing the soup in convenient-sized portions.

6 months

MUFFIN PIZZAS

Children love pizzas and they make great finger food. English muffins are used as the base for these simple pizzas but you could also use pitta bread or rolls. Why not add your favourite toppings too.

1 Preheat the grill to medium. Mix together the passata (if using canned tomatoes, mash them with a fork until fairly smooth), pesto or paste, olive oil and oregano, if using to create a sauce.

2 Cover the top of each muffin half with half of the tomato sauce.

3 Top with a slice of mozzarella then grill for about 8–10 minutes, or until the cheese has melted and is slightly golden. Cut each muffin half into quarters to make them more manageable to eat and leave to cool to the right temperature.

1–2 child-size servings

vegetable fingers

INGREDIENTS

2 tbsp passata (smooth tomato sauce) or canned chopped tomatoes
1 tsp tomato pesto or paste
½ tsp olive oil
Pinch of dried oregano (optional)
1 English muffin, halved horizontally
2 slices mozzarella, drained, patted dry

Note Tomato pesto contains pinenuts, which are not recommended for babies with a family history of nut allergy.

8 months

MINI QUICHES

These baby-sized pies are just the right size for small hands to handle. Here, puff pastry is used but you could use flaky pastry, if preferred.

3–6 child-size servings

salad or vegetables and new potatoes

INGREDIENTS

Butter, for greasing
200g ready-rolled puff pastry,
    defrosted if frozen
3 medium eggs, beaten
125ml milk
55g mature Cheddar cheese,
    grated
1 medium tomato, sliced

1 Preheat the oven to 200°C (400°F). Grease a deep six-hole muffin tin. Roll out the puff pastry until it is quite thin and press it into the six muffin holes. Trim the tops and chill the pastry for 30 minutes.

2 Combine the beaten eggs, milk and cheese, reserving a little cheese for sprinkling. Pour the mixture into the muffin tin and top each pie with a slice of tomato, then sprinkle with the reserved cheese.

3 Bake for 20–25 minutes until risen and golden. Leave to cool slightly before removing the pies from the tin.

12 months

BABY FALAFEL BURGERS

These nutritious burgers are made from chickpeas, which are a good source of iron, zinc, folate and vitamin E.

1 Place the chickpeas, spring onions, garlic, cumin and coriander in a food processor and blend. Add the egg and blend again until the mixture forms a coarse paste. Then place the mixture in the refrigerator for one hour.

2 Remove the chickpea paste from the refrigerator and, with floured hands, form into six burgers, about 6 cm in diameter. Roll each one in flour until lightly coated.

3 Heat enough oil to cover the base of a large frying pan. Cook the burgers (in batches and adding more oil, if necessary) for 6 minutes, turning once, until golden.

4 Serve each burger in a mini bread roll with slices of cucumber and tomato, with a dollop of humous, mayonnaise or ketchup. Or, to serve as finger food, cut the burger and roll into pieces and serve the humous, mayonnaise or ketchup on the side as a dip.

STORAGE TIP
The Baby Falafel Burgers can be frozen cooked or uncooked. Store them with a sheet of baking paper between each burger and then stacked into a pile. Put them in a freezer bag for future use.

6 burgers

1 burger will serve an eight month old **cucumber and tomato slices and humous, mayonnaise or low-sugar ketchup**

INGREDIENTS

400g can chickpeas, drained
  and rinsed
3 spring onions, chopped
2 cloves garlic, crushed
1 tsp ground cumin
1 tsp ground coriander
1 egg, beaten
Flour, for dusting
Vegetable oil, for frying
6 mini bread rolls or pittas

8-9
months

MOZZARELLA TORTILLA PARCEL

A great alternative to the usual cheese sandwich, this crispy, warm tortilla is filled with melted mozzarella, pesto and tomato – any fillings can be used, depending on what you have to hand. Serve with slices of carrot and cucumber.

 1–2 child-size servings

 slices of carrot and cucumber

INGREDIENTS

2 slices mozzarella
1 soft tortilla
2 slices tomato
1 tsp pesto
1 tsp olive oil

1 Place the mozzarella in the centre of the tortilla. Top with the slices of tomato and the pesto. Fold in the sides of the tortilla to make a square parcel.

2 Heat the oil in a heavy-based frying pan with a lid. Place the parcel seam-side down in the frying pan. Cover the pan and fry over a low heat for about 3 minutes, turning once, until golden. Halve diagonally and serve.

BABY BREADS

Tempt your baby with an out-of-the ordinary sandwich. All babies enjoy bread cut into shapes or into strips then rolled around a filling, but you also can make use of the variety of mini breads and rolls available. Pittas and bagels are available in small sizes as are many shaped rolls. They also can be bought as wholewheat versions. Croissants, too, can be found in smaller sizes and make delicious and easy-to-hold sandwich bases.

Note *Pesto contains pinenuts, which are not recommended for babies with a family history of nut allergy.*

 12 months

EGG ROLLS

This speedy dish of scrambled egg in a tortilla is a good source of iron, B vitamins and phosphorus. If your baby has difficulty holding the roll, serve the egg separately and cut the tortilla into strips; this would be suitable for babies from seven to eight months..

1 Heat the butter and oil in a heavy-based saucepan, add the pepper and spring onion. Cook for 5 minutes until softened.

2 Beat together the eggs and milk and pour the mixture into the pan. Using a wooden spoon, stir constantly, to ensure the egg doesn't stick. Continue to cook the egg, stirring, for about 4 minutes until there is no trace of runniness.

3 Remove from the heat – the egg will keep warm due to the heat from the pan. Warm the tortillas in an oven or a dry frying pan, then spoon the scrambled egg on top and roll up. Cut in half horizontally and serve.

2–4 child-size servings

on their own

INGREDIENTS

Knob of unsalted butter
1 tsp olive oil
¼ red pepper, deseeded and
   diced
1 spring onion, finely chopped
4 eggs, lightly beaten
2 tbsp milk
2 soft tortillas

12 months

TUNA TORTILLA MELT

Tuna is one of the oily fish family providing omega-3 fats, essential for brain development and function. Although canned tuna is lower in these beneficial oils than fresh tuna, it still provides useful amounts as well as valuable protein. Soft, floury tortillas are perfect for filling with all manner of healthy goodies.

 1–2 child-size servings

 steamed carrots and sweetcorn

INGREDIENTS

100g canned tuna in spring
water or olive oil, drained
1 large soft tortilla
30g grated mature Cheddar
1 small tomato, deseeded and
finely chopped

1 Mash the drained tuna with a fork and arrange it in the centre of the tortilla. Top with the grated Cheddar and sliced tomato.

2 Fold in the edges of the tortilla to encase the filling. Heat a dry, non-stick frying pan over medium heat. Place the tortilla, seam-side down, in the pan and cook for 3–5 minutes until warmed through and golden. Cut in half diagonally and serve.

 12 months

QUICK & EASY SAUSAGE ROLLS

Use the best sausages that you can find and you won't be filling your children with unwanted additives. And if you're using shop-bought bottled sauces to serve, look out for the "no added sugar and salt" varieties. If your baby can't handle the roll, serve the sausages minced or finely chopped and separate from the tortilla strips, which can be served separately.

1 Preheat the grill to medium-high. Line a grill pan with foil and arrange the sausages on top. Grill the sausages until cooked through and golden.

2 Place the tortilla strips in a dry frying pan and heat until warmed through. Spread a little of the topping of your choice over the each strip and top with a sausage. Roll up each strip to encase the sausage.

1–2 child-size servings

mayonnaise, ketchup, guacamole or humous

INGREDIENTS

- 4 good quality cocktail-sized pork sausages or vegetarian alternative
- 1 small soft flour tortilla, cut into four strips

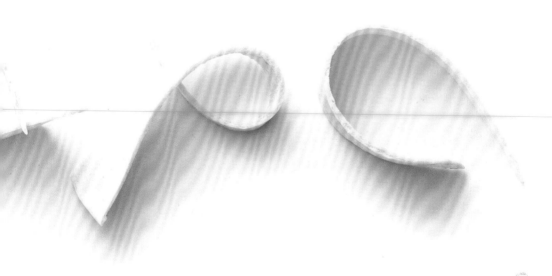

9 months

MACARONI & LEEK CHEESE

A family favourite for all ages, macaroni cheese is great comfort food and provides calcium for strong teeth and bones. Purée, mince or finely chop depending on the age of your baby.

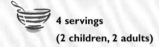

4 servings
(2 children, 2 adults)

steamed vegetables

INGREDIENTS

300g macaroni
50g butter
3 leeks, trimmed and chopped
4 tbsp plain flour
700ml milk (breast, formula, cow's or alternative)
1 heaped tsp English mustard powder
2 tbsp crème fraîche
50g Parmesan cheese, finely grated
110g mature Cheddar, grated

1 Cook the macaroni in a large saucepan of boiling water following the instructions on the packet.

2 Melt the butter in a medium-sized, heavy-based saucepan, and then add the leeks and sauté for 4 minutes until softened.

3 Stir in the flour and cook for one minute, stirring continuously. Gradually add the milk, stirring all the time with a whisk to avoid any lumps. When all of the milk has been added, stir in the mustard. Preheat the grill to high.

4 Bring the white sauce to the boil, then reduce the heat and simmer for 5 minutes, stirring frequently. Stir in the crème fraîche, half of the Parmesan and two-thirds of the Cheddar and heat through until the cheese has melted.

5 Drain the pasta, reserving three tablespoons of the cooking water. Return the pasta and water to the pan and pour in the cheese sauce. Turn until the pasta is coated in the sauce then transfer to a warm ovenproof dish.

6 Sprinkle the remaining Parmesan and Cheddar over the top and grill for 6–8 minutes until the top is golden.

VARIATION
In addition to the leeks, you could add steamed broccoli or peas and top the macaroni with slices of tomato.

STORAGE TIP
Macaroni & Leek Cheese will keep stored in the fridge in an airtight container for up to three days or can be frozen for up to three months.

6 months

POTATO, PEA & PESTO PASTA

It's a good idea to familiarise babies and young children with strong flavours and pesto is ideal for this. You could use a ready-prepared alternative, if preferred. Peas are a firm favourite with most children.

1 First make the pesto. Place the basil, garlic and pine nuts in a food processor and process until finely chopped. Gradually add the olive oil, then the Parmesan and blend to a course purée. Season to taste.

2 Cook the pasta in plenty of boiling salted water following the manufacturer's instructions, until just tender. Add the peas 2 minutes before the end of the cooking time. Drain, but leave three tablespoons of the cooking water remaining and return the pasta and peas to the saucepan.

3 Meanwhile, boil the potatoes for 10 minutes, or until tender. Drain and allow to cool slightly before cutting into bite-sized pieces.

4 Add the potatoes to the peas and pasta, and stir in half of the pesto. Add a little extra olive oil if the sauce appears dry. Stir well, but gently, until the peas and pasta are thoroughly coated, and then heat through.

5 Serve sprinkled with Parmesan cheese then purée, mince or chop as required; you may need to add a little extra water.

STORAGE TIP

Any remaining pesto can be stored in an airtight jar in the fridge for up to a week.

Note Pesto contains pine nuts – avoid serving to babies if there is a history of nut allergy, asthma, hay fever or eczema within the immediate family. Please consult your doctor.

**4 servings
(2 children, 2 adults)**

steamed broccoli

INGREDIENTS

300g pasta wheels or shape of
    your choice
75g frozen petit pois
400g baby new potatoes,
    scrubbed and halved
Olive oil, for drizzling
Freshly grated Parmesan, to
    serve

Pesto

150g fresh basil leaves, stalks
    removed
1 clove garlic, crushed
25g pine nuts
85ml olive oil
30g Parmesan cheese, freshly
    grated

8
months

SPAGHETTI WITH ROASTED BUTTERNUT SQUASH

Butternut squash has a delicious sweetness which is enhanced when roasted. This simple pasta dish is a favourite with babies and older children alike. Purée, mash or finely chop depending on the age of your baby, while the pinenuts can be finely chopped or ground.

4 servings
(2 children, 2 adults)

a green vegetable

INGREDIENTS

1 small butternut squash, peeled, deseeded and cubed
3 tbsp olive oil
2 sprigs fresh rosemary (opt ional)
300g spaghetti
1 large clove garlic, finely chopped
1 tbsp freshly chopped parsley (optional)
40g pinenuts, toasted and finely chopped (optional)
Parmesan, freshly grated, to serve

1 Preheat the oven to 200°C (400°F). Toss the butternut squash in half of the olive oil and arrange on a baking tray; place the rosemary, if using, on top. Roast the squash for 25 minutes, turning occasionally, until tender. Remove from the oven and set aside.

2 Meanwhile, cook the spaghetti in plenty of boiling water following the manufacturer's instructions. Drain, reserving two tablespoons of the cooking water, and return the pasta and water to the pan.

3 Heat the remaining olive oil in a frying pan and fry the garlic for one minute until softened, but not browned. Add the garlic and the oil to the pasta with the squash and parsley, if using. Stir well until combined and heat through.

4 Serve the pasta with a sprinkling of the toasted pinenuts, if liked, and Parmesan, if using.

STORAGE TIP
Spaghetti with Roasted Butternut Squash will keep in the fridge in an airtight container for up to two days or you can freeze it for up to three months.

6 months

Note *Contains pine nuts – avoid serving to babies if there is a history of nut allergy, asthma, hay fever or eczema within the immediate family. Please consult your doctor.*

CREAMY BROCCOLI PASTA BAKE

Broccoli contains many nutrients, including calcium, iron, zinc, B vitamins and vitamin C. It can be a real struggle to get children to eat their greens, but cutting them small and immersing them in a creamy cheese sauce seems to make them more palatable.

1 Cook the pasta in plenty of boiling, salted water according to the manufacturer's instructions. Add the broccoli and cauliflower to the pasta 5 minutes before the end of the cooking time. Drain the pasta and vegetables well and transfer to a large bowl.

2 Meanwhile, make the cheese sauce. Melt the butter in a heavy-based saucepan. Stir in the flour and cook for about 2 minutes, stirring continuously, or until the mixture forms a thick brown paste. Remove from the heat and gradually add the warm milk a little at a time, whisking well with a balloon whisk after each addition. Continue to add the milk until the cheese sauce is smooth and creamy.

3 Return the cheese sauce to the heat and add the mustard, if using, and cream cheese. Cook for about 10 minutes until the sauce has thickened. Mix in the Cheddar cheese, leaving some to sprinkle over the top of the bake, and stir well until it has melted. Pour the sauce over the pasta and vegetables in the bowl and mix gently until combined.

4 Preheat the grill to high. Transfer the pasta and vegetables to an ovenproof dish and sprinkle with more Cheddar cheese and the breadcrumbs. Grill for five to 10 minutes until the cheese is bubbling and the breadcrumbs are golden brown. Purée, mash or finely chop depending on the age of your child.

VARIATION
Instead of broccoli and cauliflower, other vegetables such as peas, carrots, leeks and green beans can be used.

4 servings
(2 children, 2 adults)

steamed carrots

INGREDIENTS
230g pasta spirals
175g broccoli, cut into small florets
85g cauliflower, cut into small florets
25g butter
3 tbsp plain flour
700ml milk, warmed
1 tbsp Dijon mustard (optional)
2 tbsp cream cheese
115g mature Cheddar cheese, grated, plus extra for sprinkling
2 tbsp fresh breadcrumbs

6 months

BABY VEGETABLE RISOTTO

Risotto is very simple to make but does require stirring time, which can be quite therapeutic after a hectic day. Purée or mash depending on your baby's age. Once your baby is 12 months, you can prepare the risotto with low-salt vegetable stock instead of water.

4 servings
(2 children, 2 adults)

steamed carrots

INGREDIENTS

2 tbsp olive oil
15g butter
4 baby leeks, sliced
4 baby courgettes, sliced
1 tsp dried oregano
250g risotto rice
1 litre water
55g petit pois
85g Parmesan cheese, grated

1 Heat the oil and butter in a large heavy-based saucepan. Add the leeks and courgettes and fry for 5 minutes or until tender. Add the oregano and rice and cook for 2 minutes, stirring continuously, until the rice is glossy and slightly translucent.

2 Add the water a ladleful at a time, stirring continuously. Wait for the water to be absorbed before adding another ladleful, continue in this way until the rice is tender and creamy but still retains a little bite – it should take about 25 minutes.

3 Add the peas, the last spoonful of water and three-quarters of the Parmesan cheese and stir well. Sprinkle with the remaining Parmesan just before serving.

6
months

PESTO & PEA RISOTTO

Pesto is a popular sauce served with pasta but it works equally well stirred into rice or spooned over baked potatoes. To make your own, see recipe on page 95. Risotto is a great dish for babies and one that is relatively easy for them to serve themselves. Once your baby is 12 months, you can use low-salt vegetable stock instead of water.

4 servings
(2 children, 2 adults)

grilled tomatoes

1 | Heat the water in a saucepan and add half of the peas. When cooked, scoop out the peas using a slotted spoon and transfer to a blender with a ladleful of water. Blend the peas until puréed and set aside.

2 | Heat the oil and butter in a large heavy-based saucepan and fry the onions over a low heat for 10 minutes until softened. Add the garlic and fry for another minute.

3 | Pour in the rice and stir until it is coated in the onion mixture. Add a ladleful of water and simmer, stirring, until the liquid is absorbed. Continue to add water, a ladleful at a time, until the liquid is almost fully absorbed and the rice is tender and creamy in texture; this will take about 20–25 minutes.

4 | Stir in the pea purée, pesto and half of the Parmesan and heat though. Season with pepper, if using, and serve sprinkled with the remaining Parmesan.

STORAGE TIP
Pesto & Pea Risotto will keep stored in the fridge in an airtight container for up to two days or can be frozen for up to three months. Reheat thoroughly -- you may need to add a little water – before serving.

INGREDIENTS
1 litre water
250g frozen petit pois
1 tbsp olive oil
20g butter
2 onions, finely chopped
2 large cloves garlic, finely
  chopped
250g risotto rice
6 tbsp pesto
50g Parmesan cheese, finely
  grated
Freshly ground black pepper
  (optional)

Note *Pesto contains pine nuts; avoid serving to babies if there is a history of nut allergy, asthma, hay fever or eczema within the immediate family. Please consult your doctor.*

MEXICAN RICE

This nutritionally balanced, lightly spiced meal is delicious topped with grated Cheddar cheese or a spoonful of guacamole or humous. Brown rice is more nutritious than white but is also higher in fibre, so you may prefer to substitute white rice here.

4 servings
(2 children, 2 adults)

nacho chips; no-salt
variety is preferred

INGREDIENTS

175g brown rice, rinsed
½ low-salt vegetable stock
  cube (optional)
55g fine green beans, sliced
1 large carrot, finely diced
1 tsp ground cumin (optional)
½ tsp mild curry powder
  (optional)
200g can kidney beans,
  drained and rinsed
6 medium tomatoes, halved
  and deseeded
1 onion, sliced
2 cloves garlic, unpeeled
1 tbsp olive oil
grated Cheddar cheese, to
  serve

1 Preheat the oven to 180°C (350°F). Place the rice in a saucepan and cover with water (the water level should be about 2 cm above the rice). Add the stock cube, if using, then bring to the boil. Reduce the heat, cover and simmer for 30 minutes, or until the rice is tender.

2 Add the green beans, carrot, spices (if using) and kidney beans and stir thoroughly. Cook for a further five to 10 minutes, or until all of the water has been absorbed. Remove from the heat and leave to stand, covered, for 5 minutes.

3 Meanwhile, place the tomatoes, onion and garlic in a baking dish and toss them in the oil until thoroughly coated. Roast for 20 minutes, or until the tomatoes are tender. Transfer to a blender or food processor and purée.

4 Add the tomato purée to the rice-and-bean mixture and stir until mixture is thoroughly coated. Sprinkle with grated Cheddar cheese and serve.

12 months

VEGETABLE FINGERS

These vegetarian alternatives to fish fingers are dipped in polenta, which gives them a delicious golden crispy coating, but you could use fresh breadcrumbs instead. The fingers are a useful way of disguising vegetables if your child dislikes anything remotely green. Finely chopped broccoli, grated cabbage, finely chopped carrots or green beans can also be used.

1 Cook the potatoes in plenty of boiling water for about 10–15 minutes, or until tender. Add the peas 2 minutes before the end of the cooking time. Drain the vegetables well and leave them to cool.

2 While the potatoes and peas are cooking, steam the leeks for 5–8 minutes, or until tender. Squeeze the leeks to get rid of any excess water and combine with the potatoes and peas. Mash well. Leave to cool completely. When the mixture is cool, stir in the cheese.

3 Sprinkle the polenta on a plate until covered. Take two large tablespoonfuls of the potato mash and, using your hands, form them into a "finger" shape. Roll each finger in the polenta and turn until completely coated. Continue until you have used up all of the potato mixture.

4 Heat enough oil to cover the bottom of a heavy-based frying pan. Cook the fingers in batches for 3 minutes on each side, or until heated through and golden.

2–4 child-size servings

steamed peas and carrots

INGREDIENTS

450g potatoes, cut into chunks
55g frozen peas
1 leek, finely chopped
85g canned no-sugar or salt sweetcorn, drained
55g mature Cheddar cheese, grated
Fine polenta or cornmeal, for coating
Vegetable oil, for frying

8 months

SWEET POTATO BAKE

This delicious pie is simple comfort food and just the thing for a cold winter's night. It is an attractive, colourful dish, made with vibrant orange layers of sweet potatoes and a bright green layer of leeks, spinach and peas. Purée, mash or mince depending on the age of your baby.

4 servings

(2 children, 2 adults)

low-sugar and salt baked beans

INGREDIENTS

675g potatoes, peeled and diced

350g sweet potatoes, peeled and diced (use the orange-flesh variety)

2 tbsp olive oil

1 large leek, finely chopped

1 tbsp dried oregano or thyme

140g spinach, stalks removed and chopped (optional)

115g frozen petit pois

55g unsalted butter, plus extra for greasing

150ml milk, warmed

2 tbsp double cream (optional)

1 tbsp Dijon mustard

85g Cheddar cheese, grated

1 Preheat the oven to 200°C (400°F). Cook the potatoes and sweet potatoes in plenty of boiling salted water for 15–20 minutes, or until tender.

2 Meanwhile, heat the oil in a heavy-based frying pan and fry the leek for 5 minutes until softened. Add the oregano or thyme and the spinach (if using) then cook for a further 3 minutes. Stir in the peas and remove from the heat.

3 Drain the potatoes well and add the butter, warmed milk, cream (if using) and mustard. Mash the potatoes well until smooth and creamy. Butter an ovenproof dish and spoon half of the mash into the dish. Smooth with the back of a spoon and top with the leek mixture. Spoon the rest of the mash over the top of the leeks and sprinkle with the Cheddar cheese. Bake the pie for 20 minutes until golden.

6 months

ROASTED VEGETABLE TART

If it's a struggle to get your children to eat vegetables, this delicious tart is the answer since the roasted vegetables are puréed until they are smooth and creamy. It makes a delicious alternative to a Sunday roast.

1 Preheat the oven to 200°C (400°F). Place the squash, garlic, onions and pepper in a roasting dish. Toss in the oil and top with the fresh herbs, then roast for 20 minutes.

2 Remove from the oven and add the tomatoes. Turn the vegetables in the oil and return to the oven for a further 15 minutes, or until tender.

3 Remove the fresh herbs and garlic and discard. Put the tomatoes into a food processor, along with the rest of the vegetables. Blend until smooth, then leave the mixture to cool.

4 Lay the sheet of puff pastry on a baking sheet. Brush the edge of the pastry with egg, then fold over to make a lip and seal with your fingers. Spoon the roasted vegetable mixture over the pastry, leaving a gap around the edge.

5 Sprinkle with the cheese. Brush the folded edge of the pastry with egg and bake for 15 minutes until the pastry has risen and is golden.

VARIATION

Serve the vegetable mixture combined with rice or pasta (omitting the pastry) and sprinkle with a little grated Cheddar cheese.

4 servings
(2 children, 2 adult)

roast potatoes and
steamed vegetables

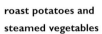

INGREDIENTS

450g butternut squash, peeled, deseeded and cubed
2 cloves garlic
2 red onions, quartered
I red pepper, cored, deseeded and cut into large slices
3 tbsp olive oil
2 sprigs fresh rosemary
3 sprigs fresh basil
3 tomatoes, halved and deseeded
425g packet ready-rolled puff pastry, defrosted, if necessary
I egg, beaten, to glaze
55g Cheddar cheese, grated

LENTIL DAHL

Children often like stronger flavours than adults give them credit for, and it's a good idea to familiarise infants with new tastes. The lentil is much underrated but this low-fat, protein-rich pulse provides iron, folic acid and zinc as well as fibre, and its mild flavour combines well with spices. Adults may like to add a chopped fresh chilli.

**4 servings
(2 children, 2 adults)**

basmati rice, naan bread or a similar Indian flatbread and a green vegetable.

INGREDIENTS

2 tbsp sunflower oil
1 large onion, chopped
2 large cloves garlic, crushed
4 cardamom pods, split
2 bay leaves
2 carrots, grated
2 tbsp grated fresh ginger
2 tsp ground coriander
200g red split lentils
500ml water
200ml reduced-fat coconut milk
200ml passata or canned chopped tomatoes
2 tsp garam masala
Juice of 1 lime
4 tbsp chopped fresh coriander (optional)

1 Heat one tablespoon oil in a large, heavy-based saucepan and sauté the onion for 10 minutes, or until softened, stirring frequently. Add the garlic and sauté for another 30 seconds, stirring, followed by the cardamom, bay leaves, carrots, ginger and ground coriander.

2 After one minute, add the lentils, water, coconut milk and passata to the pan, stir, and bring to the boil, then reduce the heat and simmer, covered, for 20 minutes. Stir in the garam masala and lime juice and cook, covered, for another 20 minutes, stirring occasionally.

3 When the lentils are tender, remove the pan from the heat and remove the whole spices then purée with a hand-held blender until smooth. Stir in the chopped coriander, if using.

STORAGE TIP

Lentil Dahl will keep stored in the fridge in an airtight container for up to five days or can be frozen for up to three months.

12 months

TOMATO & TUNA GNOCCHI

Canned tuna is a valuable source of protein and brain-boosting omega-3 essential fatty acids, albeit in lower quantities than fresh fish. Gnocchi are Italian potato dumplings and are the ultimate comfort food. This meal is so quick to prepare and delicious, it's sure to become a family favourite.

1 Heat the oil in a saucepan over a medium heat and fry the garlic for 30 seconds. Stir in the oregano then the chopped tomatoes.

2 Bring the sauce to the boil, then reduce the heat to low. Half cover the pan with a lid and simmer for about 10 minutes, or until the sauce has reduced and thickened slightly.

3 Meanwhile, bring a saucepan of water to the boil. Add the gnocchi and return the water to the boil then stir gently and cook for one minute, or as the packet directs; drain.

4 Stir the tuna into the tomato sauce. Half-cover the pan with a lid and heat through gently for 2 minutes, stirring the sauce occasionally.

5 Return the gnocchi to the saucepan and pour in enough tuna sauce to coat, turning it until covered. To serve to babies of six months, purée the dish and add a little extra water.

STORAGE TIP
Home-made tomato sauce (without tuna) is a useful standby and can be kept in the fridge in an airtight container for up to one week or frozen for up to three months. The complete dish will keep chilled for up to two days and can be reheated before serving.

4 servings
(2 children, 2 adults)

a salad or green
vegetable

INGREDIENTS

1 tsp olive oil
2 cloves garlic, finely chopped
1 tsp dried oregano (optional)
400g can chopped tomatoes
  or passata
1 tbsp tomato purée
200g can tuna in olive oil,
  drained
Packaged gnocchi (for the
  children, 12–20 depending
  on ages, plus extra for
  adults)

6 months

TUNA & LEEK FRITTATA

A protein-rich, nutritious dish, this Spanish-style tortilla can be eaten hot or cold and makes a great family dish as well as finger food. If your baby is unable to handle finger food, mince or finely chop.

 **4 servings
(2 children, 2 adults)**

 **potato wedges and
vegetable sticks**

INGREDIENTS

1 tbsp olive oil
small knob of butter
1 large leek, finely sliced
200g can tuna in olive oil or
   spring water, drained
6 eggs, beaten

1 Heat the oil and butter in a medium-sized, ovenproof frying pan then fry the leek for 5–7 minutes, or until softened. Stir in the tuna, making sure that there is an even distribution of leek and tuna and that some chunks of tuna remain.

2 Preheat the grill to medium-high. Pour the eggs evenly over the tuna and leek mixture. Cook over a moderate heat for 5 minutes, or until the eggs are just set and the base of the frittata is golden brown.

3 Place the pan under the grill and cook the top of the frittata for three minutes or until set and lightly golden. Serve the frittata warm or cold, cut into wedges or fingers.

VARIATION
Try adding 200g cooked diced chicken or four rashers grilled bacon instead of the tuna. Cooked, sliced sausages (about four) or 200g diced smoked ham could also be used in place of the tuna.

**8
months**

PLAICE WITH ROASTED TOMATOES

If serving to babies as a purée, peel off the skin from the fish after cooking and flake taking care to remove any bones before combining with the roasted tomatoes and a little water or milk. You could use any type of fish in this recipe.

1 Preheat the oven to 200°C (400°F). Heat one tablespoon of the oil in a roasting tin and add the tomatoes and basil. Turn the tomatoes in the oil and season with pepper, if using. Roast for six to 10 minutes until tender. Peel off the tomato skins.

2 Dust the fish in seasoned flour. Heat half of the butter and a little of the remaining oil in a frying pan until very hot. Cook two fillets for 4–5 minutes, turning halfway. Keep warm while you cook the remaining plaice.

3 Place the fish on serving plates with the tomatoes and squeeze over the lemon juice, if using.

4 servings
(2 children, 2 adults)

potato wedges and peas

INGREDIENTS

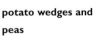

1½ tbsp olive oil, plus extra
   for frying
20 cherry tomatoes
Handful fresh basil
4 plaice fillets
Flour, for dusting
20g unsalted butter
2 tsp lemon juice (optional)

6 months

CREAMY FISH PIE

Perfect comfort food, this complete meal provides a good balance of nutrients such as low-fat protein, vitamin C, B vitamins, zinc and calcium. It's also a great meal for children but make sure there are no bones in the dish. For babies under 12 months, omit the prawns.

4 servings
(2 children, 2 adults)

steamed broccoli or
green beans

INGREDIENTS

2 tbsp vegetable oil
1 small leek, sliced
 or 1 onion, chopped
1 stick celery, chopped
1 carrot, chopped
1 bay leaf
700g potatoes, peeled and
 halved or quartered, if large
25g butter, plus extra for
 topping
2 tbsp plain flour
300ml milk
1 tsp Dijon mustard
2 tbsp crème fraîche
250g undyed smoked haddock
 fillet or similar smoked fish,
 skinned and cut into 2.5cm
 pieces
250g haddock fillet or similar
 firm white fish, skinned and
 cut into 2.5 cm pieces
100g small cooked prawns,
 defrosted if frozen
 (optional)
100g frozen petit pois

1 Heat the oil in a large saucepan and fry the leek, celery and carrot for 10 minutes until softened. Add the bay leaf while the vegetables are cooking.

2 Meanwhile, cook the potatoes in plenty of boiling water until tender, and then drain well. Preheat the oven to 180°C (350°F).

3 Mash the potatoes with the butter until smooth – you want quite a dry mash. Cover the pan with a lid to keep the mash warm and set aside.

4 Stir the flour into the softened onions and cook for one minute then gradually add the milk, stirring continuously. When the sauce has thickened, stir in the mustard and crème fraîche and heat through.

5 Add the fish, prawns and peas to the white sauce and stir until combined then spoon the mixture into an ovenproof dish.

6 Top the fish mixture with the mashed potato in an even layer. Dot the top with little knobs of butter then bake for about 25 minutes until golden.

STORAGE TIP
Creamy Fish Pie (without prawns) will keep stored in the fridge in an airtight container for up to three days or can be frozen for up to three months.

SALMON FINGERS WITH SWEET POTATO CHIPS

This healthy version of the children's classic fish fingers and chips offers plenty of brain-boosting omega-3 fatty acids. Children need essential fatty acids provided by the salmon for their rapidly developing brains and nerves. If your baby is unable to handle the fingers, mash or cut into smaller pieces as appropriate.

1 Preheat the oven to 200°C (400°F). To make the chips, dry the sweet potatoes on a clean tea towel. Spoon the oil into a roasting tin and heat briefly. Toss the sweet potatoes in the warm oil until covered and roast for 30 minutes, turning them half-way through, until tender and golden.

2 Meanwhile, mix together the cornmeal or polenta with the Parmesan on a plate. Dip each salmon finger into the beaten egg then roll them in the cornmeal and Parmesan mixture until evenly coated.

3 Heat enough oil to cover the base of a large heavy-based frying pan. Carefully arrange the salmon fingers in the pan and cook them for six minutes, turning half-way through, until golden. Drain on kitchen paper then serve with the sweet potato chips.

VARIATION
Try using thick fillets of white fish such as cod, haddock, pollack or hoki in place of the salmon.

4 servings
(2 children, 2 adults)

peas and carrots

INGREDIENTS

100g fine cornmeal, polenta or fresh breadcrumbs
3 tbsp freshly grated Parmesan
350g salmon fillet, skinned and sliced into 10 chunky fingers
2 eggs, beaten
sunflower oil, for frying
Pepper, to taste (optional)

Sweet potato chips
500g sweet potato, scrubbed and cut into wedges
2 tbsp olive oil

8 months

SALMON FRITTATA

It is recommended that children have at least two portions of fish a week, one of which should be an oily variety such as salmon. Frittata is a versatile dish and makes a nutritious lunch or supper. Alternatively, cut into wedges and serve as a snack to be eaten with fingers.

4 servings
(2 children, 2 adults)

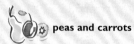 peas and carrots

INGREDIENTS

350g potatoes, peeled and
  halved
1½ tbsp olive oil
2 onions, sliced
418g can salmon, skin and
  large bones removed and
  fish flaked
2 tbsp chopped fresh parsley
  (optional)
6 eggs, lightly beaten
Freshly ground black pepper
  (optional)
25g unsalted butter

1 Cook the potatoes in plenty of boiling water until tender. Drain the potatoes and set aside.

2 Meanwhile, heat the oil in a large heavy-based frying pan with an ovenproof handle. Sauté the onions over a low heat for 10 minutes, or until softened.

3 Slice the potatoes into rounds and put into a large mixing bowl with the salmon, onions, parsley, if using, and eggs. Stir the mixture gently until combined then carefully pour it into the frying pan. Season with pepper, if using.

4 Preheat the grill to medium. Cook the frittata over a medium-low hob until the base has set and is slightly golden – about 3 minutes.

5 Place the pan under the preheated grill for about 2 minutes until the frittata is slightly golden and set.

VARIATION
Try using canned tuna in spring water, drained, in place of the salmon.

STORAGE TIP
Salmon Frittata will keep stored in the fridge for up to two days.

12
months

VEGETABLE SOUP WITH CHICKEN DUMPLINGS

Some children like to be able to identify what they are eating so are happy to try pieces of vegetable and the like, while others are more likely to eat up if the dish is puréed; this soup can be served either way. For babies of six months, purée the dumplings with the soup.

1 To make the chicken dumplings, put the chicken, Parmesan, oil and breadcrumbs in a food processor or blender and process to a coarse paste. Season with pepper, if using, and form into 12 walnut-sized balls. Put the balls on a plate and chill, covered, for 30 minutes until they firm up.

2 Heat the oil in a large saucepan and sauté the onion for 5 minutes, stirring frequently, until softened. Next, add the celery, carrots, potatoes, bay leaves and sauté for a further 2 minutes.

3 Pour in the water and add the bouquet garni then bring up to the boil. Reduce the heat and simmer the soup, half-covered, for 10 minutes.

4 Add the chicken balls and cook them for about 5–8 minutes, turning them occasionally, until they are cooked through and the soup has reduced slightly.

5 Remove the chicken dumplings with a slotted spoon and set aside. Stir the crème fraîche into the soup and heat through gently. Purée the soup in a blender, if preferred, then season to taste with pepper, if using.

5 Ladle the soup into four bowls then distribute the dumplings as appropriate, mincing or chopping them, if necessary.

STORAGE TIP
The Vegetable Soup will keep stored in the fridge in an airtight container for up to five days or can be frozen for up to three months. The cooked dumplings can be kept in the fridge for up to two days or frozen for up to three months.

4 servings
(2 children, 2 adults)

bread

INGREDIENTS
1 tbsp olive oil
1 large onion, chopped
1 stick celery, diced
2 large carrots, scrubbed and diced
2 large potatoes, peeled and diced
2 bay leaves
1.25 litres water
1 sachet bouquet garni
2 tbsp crème fraîche (optional)
Freshly ground black pepper (optional)

Chicken dumplings
300g skinless chicken breasts, cubed
20g Parmesan cheese, finely grated
1½ tbsp olive oil
20g fresh breadcrumbs
Freshly ground black pepper (optional)

8 months

BARBECUE CHICKEN WITH COLESLAW

It's a good idea to familiarise children with new and stronger flavours when young so they are less likely to become fussy eaters later in life. This barbecue marinade gives the chicken a wonderful colour and sweet-sour taste.

4 servings
(2 children, 2 adults)

in place of the coleslaw you could serve the chicken with steamed broccoli, carrots and new potatoes

INGREDIENTS

4 skinless, boneless chicken
  breasts

Marinade
3 tbsp tomato ketchup
2 tbsp soy sauce
2 tbsp balsamic or sherry
  vinegar
2 tbsp maple syrup

Coleslaw
2 tbsp grated carrot
2 tbsp grated white cabbage
1 tsp mayonnaise
2 tsp natural yoghurt
squeeze of lemon juice
1 tsp olive oil

1 Mix together the ketchup, soy sauce, vinegar and maple syrup in a shallow dish. Add the chicken and turn until the breasts are coated in the barbecue sauce. Marinate the chicken for 30 minutes, or longer if you have time, turning the meat occasionally.

2 Meanwhile, preheat the grill to medium-high and line the grill pan with foil.

3 Grill the chicken for about 20 minutes, turning once, and spooning over more marinade, until cooked through. Discard any leftover marinade.

4 While the chicken is cooking, prepare the coleslaw. Put the grated carrots and cabbage into a bowl. Mix in the mayonnaise, yoghurt, lemon juice and olive oil then stir until everything is mixed together.

5 Remove the cooked chicken from the grill and leave to cool slightly. Cut the chicken into pieces if your baby is able to handle finger foods or if he or she is not ready, mince or finely chop the chicken. Accompany with the coleslaw.

STORAGE TIP
The cooked chicken will keep chilled for up to two days. Store the coleslaw in an airtight container for up to three days.

8-9 months

CHICKEN STICKS

Chicken is an excellent source of low-fat protein but try to buy organic, free-range meat, if possible. Remove the skewers before serving to babies. If your baby is unable to handle finger foods, purée, mince or finely chop depending on his or her age.

1 Soak 16 wooden skewers in a bowl of water for 30 minutes to prevent them burning. Cut each chicken breast lengthways into four strips and thread each one on to a skewer.

2 Combine the olive oil, lemon juice and pepper, if using, in a small bowl then brush the chicken with the mixture.

3 Heat a griddle pan or grill to medium-hot. Cook the chicken skewers for 3 minutes on each side until golden and cooked through, making sure there is no trace of pink inside. Cook for slightly longer if there is any sign of pink.

**4 servings
(2 children, 2 adults)**

couscous or rice and sweetcorn

INGREDIENTS

4 skinless, boneless chicken
 breasts
2 tbsp olive oil
juice of ½ lemon
Pepper to taste (optional)

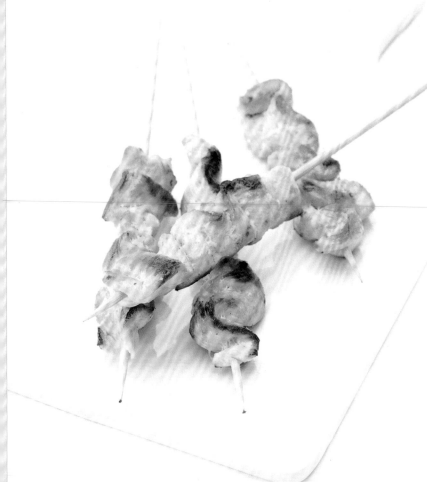

6-7
months

TURKEY PATTIES WITH PINEAPPLE RELISH

These patties are made with low-fat turkey and little else. Turkey provides useful amounts of protein and B vitamins and is generally lower in fat than red meat. The patty comes with a vitamin C-rich pineapple and mint relish.

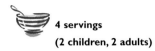

4 servings
(2 children, 2 adults)

vegetable sticks

INGREDIENTS

300g free-range lean turkey
  mince
1 tsp dried oregano
1 large garlic clove, crushed
  (optional)
Freshly ground black pepper,
  to taste (optional)
Olive oil, for brushing
Burger buns or rolls, to serve;
  use mini rolls for children

Pineapple relish
15g canned or fresh peeled
  pineapple, finely diced
1 tbsp finely finely chopped
  fresh mint (optional)
4 cm piece cucumber, peeled,
  seeded and finely diced
2 tsp lemon juice

1 Mix together the minced turkey, oregano and garlic, if using, in a mixing bowl. Season with pepper, if using, and divide the mixture into portions. Use your hands to roll each portion into a ball then flatten into a patty shape. Put the patties on a plate, cover with cling film and chill for 30 minutes.

2 Preheat the grill to medium-high and line the grill pan with foil. Meanwhile, mix together the ingredients for the relish and set aside to allow the flavours to mingle.

3 Brush the patties with oil then grill them for 3–5 minutes each side, or until cooked through and there is no trace of pink in the centre.

4 To serve, cut the buns in half crossways and put a patty on top. Add a spoonful of the relish. Top with the second half of ther bun.

SERVING TIP
If your baby can manage finger food, cut the patty into pieces and the bun into strips and serve alongside. If your baby isn't ready for finger foods, purée, mash or mince together the patty and relish.

STORAGE TIP
The patties can be frozen, uncooked, for up to three months. Separate the pattiers with a small sheet of greaseproof paper to prevent them sticking together.

8 months

TURKEY FRICASSÉE

This is a satisfying and healthy combination of turkey, vegetables and beans.

1 Sprinkle the flour on a plate and season with pepper, if using. Toss the turkey pieces in the flour.

2 Heat the oil in a large heavy-based lidded sauté pan over medium heat and fry the onion for 7 minutes. Remove the onion and add the turkey pieces. Cook for 10 minutes, turning the turkey occasionally, until browned all over. (You may need to do this in two batches, adding a little extra oil if necessary.) Set the turkey aside while you cook the vegetables.

3 Return the onion to the pan and add the garlic, pepper, oregano, carrots and sweet corn and cook for 3 minutes, or until the vegetables have softened. Return the turkey to the pan.

4 Add the water and bring to the boil then reduce the heat and simmer, covered, for 15 minutes, stirring occasionally. Add the crème fraîche and beans and warm through, stirring, for a few minutes before serving. Purée, mash or mince, if necessary.

STORAGE TIP
The fricassée can be frozen in portions, if desired, for future use. It will keep for up to three months in the freezer. Alternatively, store in the fridge in an airtight container for up to two days.

**4 servings
(2 children, 2 adults)**

**rice or mashed
potatoes**

INGREDIENTS

1 tbsp plain flour
Pepper to taste (optional)
500g skinless turkey breasts,
    cut into bite-sized pieces
1 tbsp olive oil
1 large onion, finely chopped
2 garlic cloves, chopped
1 red pepper, seeded and
    diced
2 tsp dried oregano
2 carrots, finely diced
2 corn-on-the-cobs, kernels
    sliced off
200ml water
4 tbsp crème fraîche
200g canned flageolet beans,
    drained and rinsed

8
months

MEATY PAELLA

Paella rice is perfect for young children as it has a soft, melt-in-the-mouth texture. The rice is coloured with a pinch of saffron, but you could use turmeric instead.

4 servings

(2 children, 2 adults)

steamed broccoli

INGREDIENTS

2 tbsp olive oil

1 onion, diced

1 red pepper, cored, deseeded and diced

2 cloves garlic, finely chopped

2 tomatoes, deseeded and diced

Pinch of saffron

650ml hot water

225g paella rice

70g frozen peas

3 frankfurters, cooked and sliced or finely chopped

1 Heat the oil in a large frying pan. Add the onion and fry for 8 minutes, or until softened. Add the pepper and garlic and cook for a further 2 minutes over a medium heat.

2 Add the tomatoes, saffron and water to the pan. Stir in the rice and bring to the boil, stirring frequently. Reduce the heat and simmer for 20 minutes, stirring occasionally, until the rice is tender and the water has been absorbed.

3 Stir in the peas and cooked frankfurters and cook for 2 minutes, or until heated through.

VARIATION

Try adding 300g cooked diced chicken or ham instead of the frankfurters.

STORAGE TIP

Store Meaty Paella in the fridge for up to two days or freeze for up to three months. Reheat until piping hot throughout.

8 months

SAUSAGE & POTATO ROAST

There is something very comforting about a roast dinner. This weekday version doesn't skimp on the comfort element but it is a more simple to prepare and cook.

1 Preheat the oven to 200°C (400°F). Place the oil in a large roasting tin with the potatoes. Turn the potatoes in the oil and roast in the oven for 10 minutes.

2 Add the sausages, squash and herbs and stir everything together and return to the oven for 15 minutes. Combine the hot water and cornflour in a jug and pour over the sausage mixture.

3 Cook for a further 10 minutes until the liquid has thickened and formed a gravy and the sausages and vegetables are cooked and golden. Remove the herbs and serve.

VARIATION

For a vegetarian version, use non-meat sausages or alternatively increase the quantity of vegetables. You could use onion, parsnip, celeriac, swede or beetroot.

4 servings
(2 children, 2 adults)

green vegetables

INGREDIENTS

2 tbsp olive oil
8 good quality pork sausages
   or vegetarian alternative
4 potatoes, cut into chunks
300g butternut squash, peeled,
   deseeded and cut into
   chunks the same size as the
   potatoes
2 sprigs fresh rosemary
2 sprigs fresh oregano
10 cherry tomatoes
150ml low-salt stock
3 tsp cornflour
Pepper, to taste (optional)

12 months

HAM & PEA PENNE

Try to buy good quality ham to give the best flavour to this quick and simple pasta dish. Ham can be quite salty so please look for reduced-salt versions if serving this dish to young babies or only serve in small quantities.

**4 servings
(2 children, 2 adults)**

steamed green vegetables

INGREDIENTS

300g penne

1 tbsp olive oil

2 large cloves garlic, chopped

200ml water

150g frozen petit pois

6 tbsp creme fraîche

4 thick slices of cured ham,
    cut into bite-sized pieces

Pepper, to taste (optional)

Freshly grated Parmesan, to
    serve

1 Cook the pasta in plenty of boiling water, following the packet instructions. Drain, reserving two tablespoons of the cooking water.

2 Meanwhile, heat the olive oil in a large, heavy-based frying pan and fry the garlic for 30 seconds. Add the water, then the peas and cook over a medium-high heat for 2 minutes until the peas are cooked and the liquid has reduced.

3 Add the ham to the pan with the creme fraîche. Cook over a low heat, stirring frequently, until warmed through. Stir in the pasta and the reserved cooking water, if required, and stir gently until combined. Season with pepper, if using, and serve sprinkled with Parmesan. Purée, adding a little milk, if serving to babies.

VARIATION

Replace the ham with 200g canned tuna or salmon. You also could use fresh cooked salmon, flaked into pieces, or cooked, diced chicken.

6 months

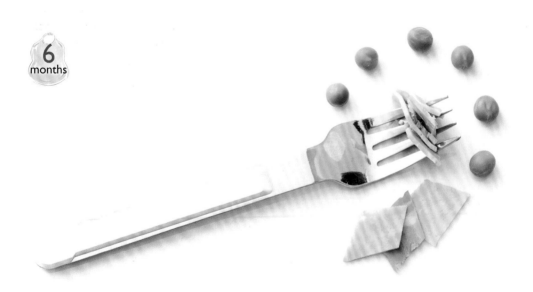

PORK WITH FRUITY COUSCOUS

The marinade gives these pork fillets a wonderful sweet, glossy glaze. A certain amount of forward planning is required as they need to marinate for at least an hour or left overnight to absorb the flavours of the marinade.

1 Mix together the ingredients for the marinade in a shallow, non-metallic dish. Add the pork fillets and turn until they coated in the marinade. Leave to marinate in the fridge for one hour, turning the pork occasionally.

2 To make the couscous, put the couscous in a heatproof bowl. Pour over boiling water until it is 5mm above the couscous; let the couscous stand until it has absorbed all of the liquid. Add a small knob of butter and fluff up with a fork. Stir in the diced nectarine and set aside.

3 Preheat the grill to high and line the grill pan with foil. Grill the pork for 10–15 minutes, turning half-way and brushing with the marinade, until cooked.

4 Serve the pork with the fruity couscous. Cut the pork into pieces or mince or coarsely chop for babies.

VARIATION
The marinade also works well with poultry, tofu and salmon.

4 servings

(2 children, 2 adults)

steamed green beans

INGREDIENTS

4 lean pork fillets

Marinade
2 tbsp runny honey
2 tbsp soy sauce
1 tbsp balsamic vinegar
1 tbsp toasted sesame oil
2 tsp olive oil

Fruity couscous
100g couscous
Small knob of butter
1 nectarine or peach, diced
2 tbsp toasted sesame seeds
2 tbsp toasted flaked almonds

12 months

PORK & APPLE PAN-FRY

Pork tenderloin is used here since it is lean and cooks quickly. The apple is perfect with pork and the beans add healthy low-fat protein and minerals.

4 servings
(2 children, 2 adults)

new potatoes or rice
and peas

INGREDIENTS

1 tbsp plain flour
1 tsp paprika
400g pork tenderloin,
    trimmed and cut into bite-
    sized pieces
1½ tbsp olive oil
1 large onion, finely chopped
1 large dessert apple, cored,
    peeled and cut into bite-
    sized pieces
1 tbsp chopped fresh
    rosemary
300ml water
2 tomatoes, deseeded and
    roughly chopped
400g can flageolet beans,
    drained and rinsed
2 tbsp crème fraîche
Pepper, to taste (optional)

1 Mix together the flour and paprika in a small plastic food bag and add the pork pieces. Shake the bag to toss the pork in the seasoned flour. Turn out the pork onto a plate, shaking off any excess flour. Alternatively, place the flour and paprika on a plate and roll the pork pieces into them to coat.

2 Heat the oil in a heavy-based frying pan, add the pork and cook for 5 minutes, turning the meat, until browned all over. Add the onion and cook for a further 7 minutes until softened. Mix in the apple and rosemary and cook for 3–4 minutes until the apples begin to break down.

3 Pour in the water, bring to the boil, then reduce the heat and simmer for 15 minutes until reduced and thickened. Stir in the tomatoes and beans then cook for another 10 minutes over a low heat. Stir in the crème fraîche and heat through before serving. Season with pepper, if using.

8
months

SPICY MINCE WITH APRICOTS

This mildly spicy dish can be made in advance and then reheated when ready to serve. The spices can be left out, if preferred, and swapped with two teaspoons dried mixed herbs.

1 Heat the oil in a large heavy-based saucepan, add the onion and cook, covered, stirring occasionally, over a medium heat for 7 minutes until softened and tender. Add the garlic, carrot, pepper and cook, covered, for a further 3 minutes.

2 Push the contents of the pan to one side and add the mince, cook, uncovered, stirring frequently until browned. Stir in the spices and cook for another minute.

3 Pour in the passata and water or stock then stir in the tomato purée and apricots. Cook, half-covered, for 30–40 minutes until reduced and thickened. If the sauce appears too liquid remove the lid or if is it too dry add a little more water or stock. Season with pepper, if using, and serve spooned over a jacket potato.

VARIATION
You can use a vegetarian alternative instead of the meat or the mince could be used as a base for cottage pie. Put the cooked mince (you could leave out the apricots) in an ovenproof dish and top with mashed potato. Cook in an oven, preheated to 200°C (400°F), for 25 minutes until golden on top.

STORAGE TIP
Store in the fridge for up to two days or freeze in portions for up to three months.

4 servings
(2 children, 2 adults)

jacket potato and green vegetables

INGREDIENTS

2 tbsp olive oil
1 onion, finely chopped
2 cloves garlic, chopped
1 carrot, grated
1 red pepper, seeded and diced
400g lean minced beef
½ tsp ground cumin
½ tsp ground cinnamon
½ tsp ground coriander
500ml passata
250ml water or low-salt vegetable stock
1 tbsp tomato purée
10 ready-to-eat unsulphured dried apricots, finely chopped
Pepper, to taste (optional)

8 months

MEAT BALLS WITH TOMATO SAUCE

Meat balls accompanied by a smooth tomato sauce are great served with vegetables or over a dish of pasta.

4 servings
(2 children, 2 adults)

pasta or steamed green vegetables, such as broccoli

INGREDIENTS

Meat balls

350g lean beef mince
1 onion, grated
1 carrot, finely grated
1 clove garlic, crushed
55g wholemeal breadcrumbs
1 small egg, beaten
1 tablespoon plain flour
Vegetable oil, for frying

Tomato sauce

1 carrot, finely chopped
1 tablespoon olive oil, plus
   extra for frying
1 clove garlic, crushed
400g can chopped tomatoes
1 tablespoon tomato purée

1 Combine the mince, onion, carrot, garlic, breadcrumbs, egg and flour in a bowl. Season to taste and place in the refrigerator for about one hour to allow the mixture to firm up.

2 To make the tomato sauce, blanch the carrots for 2–3 minutes until softened. Heat the oil in a heavy-based saucepan and fry the garlic for one minute. Add the tomatoes and purée then cook for 15 minutes until reduced and thickened. Add the carrots and heat through. Transfer to a blender or food processor and purée until smooth.

3 Form the mince mixture into walnut-sized balls using floured hands. Heat enough oil to cover the bottom of a heavy-based frying pan. Fry the balls in batches for about 10 minutes, turning occasionally, until golden.

4 Reheat the tomato sauce, if necessary, and spoon into bowls. Top with the balls and serve. If necessary, cut the balls into pieces or coarsely chop or purée in the tomato sauce.

8 months

HOMEMADE BEEF BURGERS

By using good quality, preferably organic, ingredients, you can have a healthy and delicious burger in next to no time. If your baby cannot manage finger food, serve the burger (without the bun) mashed, minced or cut up.

1 Place the oregano, onion, carrot, garlic, mince and egg in a large bowl. Season with the pepper, if using, and mix with your hands until all the ingredients are combined.

2 Divide the mixture into portions and then, using floured hands, form each portion into a burger shape. Set aside in the refrigerator for 15 minutes.

3 Heat enough oil to lightly cover the base of a large heavy-based frying pan. Place the burgers in the hot oil and fry for 5 minutes on each side until browned and cooked through.

4 Serve the burgers in buns with relish and accompaniments of choice or cut up into pieces.

**4 servings
(2 children, 2 adults)**

sliced tomato and cucumber; relish, mayonnaise, or tomato ketchup or boiled potatoes and steamed vegetables

INGREDIENTS

1 tsp dried oregano
1 onion, grated
1 carrot, finely grated
1 garlic clove, crushed
450g lean minced beef
1 small egg, beaten
Pepper to taste (optional)
Flour, for dusting
Sunflower oil, for frying
Burger buns or rolls, to serve

8 months

AUTUMN BEEF STEW

It is important to use the good quality organic beef for this hearty stew. Don't be put off by the length of time it takes to cook since it doesn't require any lengthy involvement from the cook and the slow-cooking results is a rich, thick gravy and succulent meat.

4 servings
(2 children, 2 adults)

mash and a green
vegetable

INGREDIENTS

3 tbsp flour
400–550g diced casserole beef
3 tbsp olive oil
8–10 shallots, peeled and
  halved or quartered if large
2 carrots, cut into batons
1 parsnip, sliced into rounds
2 bay leaves
1 tbsp chopped fresh
  rosemary
1 tbsp chopped fresh thyme
450ml water
250ml apple juice
1 tbsp Worcestershire sauce
200g canned chestnuts,
  drained
Pepper to taste (optional)

1 Preheat the oven to 170°C (325°F). Put the flour in a clean plastic food bag or on a plate. Toss the beef in the flour until coated. Heat one tablespoon of the oil in a large casserole dish.

2 Add one-third of the beef and cook for 5–6 minutes, turning occasionally, until browned all over – the meat may stick to the pan until it is properly sealed. Remove the browned beef from the pan and cook the remaining two batches, adding another one tablespoon oil when necessary. Set aside when all the beef has been browned.

3 Add the remaining oil to the pan with the shallots, carrots, parsnip and herbs and cook for 3 minutes, stirring occasionally.

4 Pour in the water and bring to the boil. Cook over a high heat until the liquid has reduced. Add the apple juice and Worcestershire sauce then cook for another 3 minutes.

5 Stir in the chestnuts and beef, cover the casserole dish with a lid and transfer to the oven. Cook for two hours until the stock has formed a thick, rich gravy and the meat is tender. Season with pepper, if using, before serving.

STORAGE TIP
Autumn Beef Stew will keep stored in the fridge in an airtight container for up to three days or can be frozen for up to three months.

8
months

CHINESE BEEF WITH NOODLES

Beef is a good source of iron though chicken or pork and vegetables of your choice can be used to make this speedy supper dish, if preferred. Coarsely purée, mince or finely chop all the ingredients depending on the age of your baby.

1 Heat the oil in a wok and add the beef then stir-fry over a medium-high heat for 2 minutes. Remove the beef using a slotted spoon and set aside.

2 Meanwhile, bring a large saucepan of water to the boil. Add the noodles and stir to separate them. Drain when the noodles are tender and keep them warm.

3 Add the garlic, sugar snap peas and spring onions to the wok and stir-fry for 2 minutes then return the beef to the wok with the black bean and soy sauces; stir-fry for another minute, adding a splash of water if the sauce begins to dry out.

4 Divide the noodles between the plates then top with the beef stir-fry.

STORAGE TIP

Chinese Beef with Noodles can be stored in an airtight container in the fridge for up to two days. Reheat thoroughly before serving.

4 servings
(2 children, 2 adults)

serve with a glass of fresh orange juice to enhance the absorption of the iron in the beef

INGREDIENTS

2 tbsp sunflower or vegetable oil
400–500g lean beef, cut into strips
250g medium egg noodles
3 cloves garlic
2 handfuls sugar snap peas, trimmed
1 red pepper, seeds removed and cut into 1cm strips
4 spring onions, sliced diagonally
175ml black bean sauce
2 tbsp reduced-salt soy sauce

8-9 months

FRUIT YOGURT SWIRLS

Making your own fruit yogurt couldn't be more simple and also means you know exactly what's in it. Frozen fruit – either single fruit or mixed – is an excellent alternative to fresh and still counts towards the recommended 'Five-a-day'.

1–4 child-size servings

INGREDIENTS

4 tbsp mixed red berries, defrosted if frozen

1 nectarine, halved, stoned and quartered

3–4 tbsp water

Thick natural low-fat bio yogurt, to serve

6 months

1 Put the berries, nectarine and water in a saucepan with a lid. Bring up to simmering point then cover the pan and cook for 5–7 minutes until the berries and plums are soft and beginning to break down.

2 Press the cooked fruit through a sieve to remove any seeds and skin.

3 Spoon a serving of natural yoghurt into a glass or bowl. Add a few spoonfuls of the fruit purée and swirl it into the yoghurt using a spoon handle to give a marbled effect.

STORAGE TIP
Any leftover fruit purée can be stored for up to three days in an airtight container in the fridge.

MANGO FOOL

This creamy dessert can be whipped up in a matter of minutes.

1 Place the mango in a food processor or blender, reserving four slices to decorate. Purée the mango until smooth.

2 Add the cream, sugar and yogurt and blend until combined.

3 Spoon the mixture into dessert glasses and refrigerate for one hour to firm up slightly.

VARIATION

Any of your favourite fruit can be used instead of the mango but make sure it has a soft flesh. Apples and pears or other similar fruit with a firmer flesh will need to be cooked first.

4 servings
(2 children, 2 adults)

INGREDIENTS

1 large mango, stoned, peeled and roughly chopped
200ml whipping cream
2 tsp unrefined icing sugar or fruit syrup
4 tbsp natural bio yoghurt

8 months

REAL FRUIT LOLLIES

Home-made lollies are lower in sugar than most commercially made ones and certainly free from artificial colours and other E numbers.

 6 lollies

INGREDIENTS

4 plums, halved and stoned
3 nectarines, stoned and
  roughly chopped
1 tbsp unrefined caster sugar,
  to taste
150ml ready-prepared custard

6 months

1 Put the plums and nectarines in a medium-sized, non-metallic saucepan. Add the sugar and two tablespoons water. Bring to the boil, then reduce the heat and simmer for 5 minutes until softened.

2 Leave to cool then purée until smooth – you need about 250 ml of fruit purée.

3 Combine the fruit purée and custard then spoon the mixture into six ice lolly moulds. Place in the freezer until solid.

VARIATION

Orange and mango are refreshing alternatives. Juice the fruit – you need about 400ml to make six lollies – then freeze until solid.

BANANA & MAPLE YOGURT ICE

This simple alternative to ice cream couldn't be easier to make and it's the perfect dessert for soothing sore gums and for relieving teething pain.

 1 child-size serving

INGREDIENTS

1 small ripe banana
1 heaped tbsp natural thick
  bio yogurt
1 tsp maple syrup (optional)

6 months

1 Peel the banana, wrap it tightly in plastic film and freeze until firm – at least three hours, although it can be stored in the freezer until ready to use.

2 Remove the frozen banana from the freezer and unwrap. Leave for 15 minutes to soften slightly then break into chunks.

3 Put the banana in a food processor or blender with the yogurt and maple syrup, if using, and blend until thick, smooth and creamy. Spoon the ice into a bowl.

STORAGE TIP

The Banana & Yogurt Ice will keep stored in the fridge in an airtight container for up to two days but it will defrost after an hour becoming a fruit fool. The banana can be stored in the freezer for up to three months.

STRAWBERRY SUNDAE

You can't go wrong with an ice cream sundae: this popular dessert is a breeze to make and has been adapted to ensure a healthy twist.

1 Purée the strawberries and orange juice in a food processor or blender until smooth.

2 Lightly toast the almonds or chopped nuts in a dry frying pan. Set aside.

3 To serve, place a few spoonfuls of the strawberry sauce in a tall glass. Top with a scoop of ice cream and another spoonful of sauce. Add a final scoop of ice cream. Sprinkle the nuts over the top and a few shavings of chocolate. Repeat to make another sundae.

Note This recipe contains nuts; avoid serving to babies if there is a history of nut allergy, asthma, hay fever or eczema within the immediate family. Please consult your doctor.

2 child-size servings

INGREDIENTS

125g strawberries, halved
1 tbsp fresh orange juice
1 tbsp flaked almonds or
  chopped nuts
4 scoops good quality vanilla
  ice cream
chocolate shavings, to serve
  (optional)

8 months

....

STRAWBERRY YOGURT ICE

These fruity yogurt ice lollies are particularly refreshing on a hot day and great for teething infants. Honey should not be given to infants under 12 months (see page 9).

1 Place the strawberries and yoghurt in a food processor or blender and process until smooth. Stir in the honey.

2 Pour the strawberry mixture into lolly moulds and freeze for two to three hours until solid.

4 lollies

INGREDIENTS

175g strawberries, hulled
125ml thick natural yogurt
2 tbsp clear honey

12 months

QUICK SUMMER PUDDING

This speedy version of the classic summer pudding takes a fraction of the time to prepare. It features puréed fruit for children who dislike seeds and lumps! A heart-shaped cutter is used here but you can use whatever shape you have to hand.

 **2–4 child-size servings**

INGREDIENTS

225g mixed berries, fresh or frozen
6 tbsp fresh apple juice
4 slices day-old white bread, crusts removed
Large heart-shaped cutter

1 Put the berries (reserving a few to decorate) and apple juice into a saucepan and bring to a gentle boil. Reduce the heat and simmer for 5 minutes until the fruit is soft but there is still plenty of juice.

2 Strain the juice from the fruit through a sieve into a bowl. In a separate bowl, press the fruit through the sieve using the back of a spoon – this will make a thick purée. Discard any seeds left in the sieve.

3 Cut the bread into heart shapes using a large pastry cutter – use four slices of bread to make four heart shapes. (The cutter should use as much of each slice as possible, since the bread loses its shape if it is cut too small.)

4 Place two of the hearts in a shallow dish, then spoon over the fruit purée until they are completely covered. Top the fruit soaked bread with the remaining two hearts and spoon over the juice. Press down lightly to soak the juice into the bread. Leave for 30 minutes. Decorate with the remaining berries before serving.

VARIATION

If preferred, you can leave out the bread and combine the cooked puréed berries with natural yogurt.

8 months

MIXED FRUIT COMPOTE

Many children dislike "bits" which unfortunately can put them off berries. This compote is sieved to remove an offending seeds and skin, resulting in an intensely fruity red sauce. You can buy bags of mixed frozen fruit in supermarkets.

1 Put the berries in a pan with the apple juice and water then simmer until defrosted.

2 Add the cornflour to the pan and heat gently and briefly, stirring frequently, until thickened.

3 Press the fruit through a sieve to remove any seeds or pips.

VARIATION
This fruit compote is delicious stirred into a live natural bio yogurt with a sprinkling of granola.

4–6 child-size servings

INGREDIENTS

200g frozen fruits of the forest
2 tbsp fresh apple juice
2 tbsp water
1 tsp cornflour

6 months

· ·

APPLE & CINNAMON COMPOTE

This lightly spiced apple compote makes a delicious filling for a warmed croissant. It also can be puréed and stirred into live natural bio yogurt for a healthier version of fruit yogurt.

1 Put the apple, cinnamon, butter, lemon juice (prevents the apple browning) and water in a heavy-based, non-metallic saucepan. Simmer, half-covered, over a medium heat for 15 minutes until the apples are tender.

2 Lightly mash the apples with a fork to break them down slightly or purée in a blender.

VARIATION
Pears would make a delicious alternative to the apple here, as would plums.

STORAGE TIP
Double the quantity of this recipe and freeze in convenient-sized portions for future use.

2–4 child-size servings

INGREDIENTS

2 dessert apples, cored, peeled and roughly diced
½ tsp ground cinnamon
small knob of butter
squeeze fresh lemon juice
6 tbsp water

6 months

SNOW BALLS

Packed with energy-giving and iron-boosting dried fruit and nutritious nuts and seeds, these coconut-coated balls make an excellent snack or dessert.

 **about 8 balls**

INGREDIENTS

25g hazelnuts, roughly chopped
25g whole oats
50g raisins
75g ready-to-eat dried
   unsulphured apricots, cut into
   small pieces
2 tbsp fresh orange juice
1 tbsp sunflower seeds
1 tbsp pumpkin seeds
Dessicated coconut, for coating

Note This recipe contains nuts; avoid serving to babies if there is a history of nut allergy, asthma, hay fever or eczema within the immediate family. Please consult your doctor.

1 Put the hazelnuts and oats in a dry frying pan and toast over a medium heat for 3 minutes, turning them frequently with a wooden spatula until they begin to turn golden and the oats become crisp. Leave to cool.

2 Put the raisins, apricots and orange juice into a food processor or blender and purée until the mixture becomes a smooth, thick purée. Scrape the fruit purée into a mixing bowl.

3 Put the nuts, oats and seeds in the food processor or blender and process until they are very finely chopped. Tip the mixture into the bowl with the fruit purée. Stir the fruit mixture until all the ingredients are combined.

4 Cover the bowl with cling film and chill the mixture for one hour. Scoop up a portion of the fruit and nut mixture – about the size of a walnut – in a spoon and roll it into a ball. Rolling is easier if you form it into a rough ball first then roll it in the coconut and continue to roll it.

5 Coat the ball in the desiccated coconut until it is covered then repeat to make about eight balls in total. Arrange the balls on a plate, cover loosely with cling film and chill for about 30 minutes until firmed up.

STORAGE TIP
Store Snow Balls in an airtight container for up to two weeks.

8-9 months

OAT COOKIES

These American-style cookies are packed with nutritious oats.

1 Preheat the oven to 180°C (350°F). Line two baking sheets with baking paper.

2 Beat together the butter and sugar in a mixing bowl until light and fluffy. Stir in both types of flour and the oats then mix well to make a soft dough.

3 Divide the dough into 12 pieces. Roll each piece into a ball and arrange on the baking sheets, well spaced out to allow room for the dough to spread. Flatten the top of each ball slightly and bake for 15–20 minutes until the balls are just golden but still soft in the centre.

4 Leave to cool to 5 minutes then transfer to wire racks.

12 cookies

INGREDIENTS

120g unsalted butter
75g light muscovado sugar
75g self-raising flour
25g wholemeal self-raising flour
100g whole porridge oats

12 months

PEACH CRUMBLES

This variation on the classic crumble uses whole fruits – perfect if you are just cooking for the children, since it's easier to make small portions.

 4 child-size servings

INGREDIENTS

2 peaches, halved and stone
  removed
25g plain flour
2 tbsp unsalted butter
1 tbsp porridge oats
  (optional)
2 tbsp demerara sugar

8 months

1 Preheat the oven to 180°C (350°F). Grease an ovenproof dish or baking tin and arrange the peach halves in the dish.

2 Put the flour and butter in a bowl and rub together with your fingertips to form coarse breadcrumbs. Stir in the oats and sugar and mix well.

3 Spoon the crumble mixture over the peaches and add two tablespoons of water to the dish. Bake for 25 minutes, or until the peaches are tender and the crumble slightly crisp.

VARIATION
Plums, apples, pears or nectarines make delicious alternatives to the peaches. If you have any crumble mixture left over, store it in a container or bag in the freezer for future use.

STICKY DATE CAKE

Deliciously moreish and light, this makes a great special treat pudding with custard, ice cream or yogurt or serve on its own for tea.

1 Preheat the oven to 180°C (350°F). Grease and line the base of a 20cm square cake tin with baking paper.

2 Put the dates in a medium-sized saucepan with the water. Bring to the boil then reduce the heat and simmer for about 10 minutes, or until the fruit is very soft. Purée the fruit using a hand blender.

3 Stir the bicarbonate of soda into the puréed fruit – it will froth up initially – then add the butter.

4 Meanwhile, in a large mixing bowl, whisk the eggs and sugar using an electric hand whisk for about 8 minutes until thick and creamy. Gradually sift in the flour and gently fold in using a wooden spoon. Next fold in the dried fruit mixture and vanilla.

5 Pour the cake mixture into the prepared tin and bake for 35–40 minutes, or until a skewer inserted in the middle comes out clean. Leave to stand for 10 minutes, turn out of the tin and cut into squares.

STORAGE TIP
Store the Sticky Date Cake in an airtight tin or wrapped in foil for up to one week.

about 16 squares

INGREDIENTS
200g dried soft dates, cut into small pieces
300ml water
1 tsp bicarbonate of soda
50g butter, softened, cut into small pieces
2 large free-range eggs
175g golden caster sugar
175g self-raising flour, sifted
1 tsp vanilla extract

12 months

CARROT CAKE SQUARES

Your child will never guess that this light and moist cake contains healthy carrots!

about 16 squares

INGREDIENTS

225g self-raising flour
Pinch of salt
1 teaspoon ground cinnamon
1 teaspoon ground mixed
  spice
225g light muscovado sugar
225g carrots, peeled and
  grated
3 medium eggs, lightly beaten
175ml sunflower oil

1 | Preheat the oven to 180°C (350°F). Lightly grease a 20 cm square cake tin and line the base with greaseproof paper.

2 | Sift the flour, salt and spices into a large mixing bowl. Add the sugar and carrots and mix well.

3 | Mix together the eggs and oil in a jug, then pour into the flour mixture, stirring with a wooden spoon until combined.

4 | Pour the cake mixture into the prepared cake tin and bake for 50 minutes, or until a skewer inserted into the centre of the cake comes out clean. Leave to cool for 10 minutes, and then carefully turn out the cake and leave to cool. and then cut it into small squares.

STORAGE TIP
Store the Carrot Cake Squares in an airtight tin or wrapped in foil for up to 1 week.

12 months

LEMON SPONGE PUDDINGS

These individual sponge puddings are baked rather than steamed which drastically cuts down on the cooking time without loosing any flavour.

1 Preheat the oven to 180°C (350°F). Grease six dariole moulds or ramekins and place on a baking sheet.

makes 6

2 To make the topping, mix together the golden syrup and the lemon juice with a fork.

custard

3 To make the puddings, beat the butter and sugar in a bowl until pale and fluffy. Beat in the eggs, one at a time, whisking the mixture thoroughly after each addition – the mixture may curdle but do not worry about this. Beat in the maple syrup.

INGREDIENTS

Topping
8 tbsp golden syrup
2 tbsp lemon juice

4 Add half of the flour and fold in with a metal spoon. Add the rest of the flour and fold in.

Puddings
115g softened unsalted butter, plus extra for greasing
115g soft light brown sugar
3 free-range eggs
1 tbsp maple syrup
115g self-raising flour

5 Place a spoonful of the syrup topping into each mould or ramekin, reserving about half of the mixture to serve. Spoon the sponge mixture over the topping until it nearly reaches the top and smooth the top with the back of a teaspoon. Bake for 20 minutes or until the puddings are risen and golden.

6 Remove from the oven and leave for 5 minutes, then run a knife around the edge of the moulds or ramekins to loosen the puddings. Heat the remaining syrup mixture until warm. Turn out the sponges onto serving plates and spoon over the warm syrup.

12 months

MERRY BERRY COBBLER

Berries are rich in antioxidants and vitamin C. Here, they are used as base for a warming dessert that has a delicious scone topping.

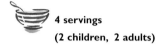

4 servings
(2 children, 2 adults)

INGREDIENTS

240g mixed berries, such as
  raspberries, blackberries,
  strawberries, blueberries,
  defrosted if frozen
8 plums, halved, stoned and
  roughly chopped
1 tsp cornflour
3 tbsp unrefined caster sugar

Topping
120g unsalted butter
2 tbsp unrefined caster sugar
200g cups plain flour
2 tsp baking powder
2 tsp cornflour
1–2 tbsp single cream

1 Preheat the oven to 180°C (350°F). Put the berries and plums in a 20 x 25 cm dish. Mix the cornflour with a little water and add to the fruit with the sugar, stir until thoroughly combined.

2 For the topping, beat the butter and sugar together until pale and fluffy. Mix in the flour, baking powder and cornflour. As the mixture becomes dry, stir in the cream to form a smooth soft dough.

3 Divide the dough into eight balls, flatten the top of each one and arrange on top of the berry mixture. Bake for 20–25 minutes until the scone topping is risen and golden.

8-9
months

APPLE & PLUM FLAPJACK PIE

Fruit crumble with a twist: this pie has a crisp nutty, oaty topping. You can vary the fruit base according to what's in season – rhubarb, nectarines, berries and pears are equally delicious. Dessert apples are used here instead of cooking apples, as they don't need so much sugar to sweeten them. Make in individual dishes or one large dish, depending what you have to hand.

1 Preheat the oven to 180°C (350°F). Toss the apples in the lemon juice to prevent them browning and arrange in a 23 cm diameter ovenproof dish with the plums; stir well to combine.

2 To make the topping, melt the syrup and butter in a heavy-based medium-sized saucepan. Remove from the heat and stir in the oats, hazelnuts and seeds. Sprinkle the mixture over the top of the fruit. Bake for 20–25 minutes until golden and beginning to crisp.

STORAGE TIP
The pie can be kept in the freezer for up to three months; defrost then reheat in the oven covered in foil. Alternatively, freeze the cooked fruit mixture and uncooked crumble mix separately and follow the recipe above for cooking instructions.

4-6 servings
(2 children, 2–4 adults)

INGREDIENTS

3 dessert apples, cored,
   peeled and diced
squeeze of lemon juice
5 plums, halved, stoned and
   diced

Topping
4 tbsp golden syrup
5 tbsp unsalted butter
150g porridge oats
2 tbsp chopped hazelnuts
2 tbsp sunflower seeds

8-9
months

INDEX

A

Additives 12
Allergies 17
Apple & Cinnamon Compote 133
Apple & Plum Flapjack Pie 141
Apple Purée 43
Apricot & Prune Fruit Spread 58
Aubergine Purée 71
Autumn Beef Stew 126
Avocado Purée 46

B

Baby Falafel Burgers 89
Baby-led weaning 13
Baby Rice 42
Baby Vegetable Risotto 98
Baked Potatoes 80
Banana & Maple Yogurt Ice 130
Banana & Strawberry Smoothie 56
Banana Purée 43
Banana Yogurt Custard 54
Barbecued Chicken with Coleslaw 112
Bean & Vegetable Mash 152
Breadsticks 74
Breakfast Omelette 62
Bubble & Squeak cakes 79

C

Carbohydrates
  Babies needs 19
  Toddlers 28
Carrot Cake Squares 138
Carrot Purée 45

Cheesy Breadsticks 74
Cheesy People 75
Chicken Balls in Tomato Sauce 115
Chicken Sticks 113
Chicken with Tomato Rice 51
Chinese Beef with Noodles 127
Chopped food 15
Chunky purée 15
Cinnamon French Toast 73
Commercial baby foods 12
Cooking for your baby 14
Country Garden Salad 76
Cream Cheese & Leek Filling 81
Creamy Broccoli Pasta Bake 97
Creamy Fish Pie 108
Creamy Guacamole 69

D

Dairy products 28
Date & Vanilla Breakfast Yogurt 57
Dried Apricot Purée 53
Drinks 16
  Stage 2 25
  From one year 32
  From two years 37

E

Eating enough 18
Egg Cups 65
Egg Rolls 91
Egg Toasts 72
Eggy Bread 64
Eggs 20
Equipment 10

F

Family meals 24
Finger foods 16
Food safety 9
Foods to avoid 9, 20
Fruit and vegetable needs
  Babies 16
  Toddlers 29
Fruit Fool 55
Fruit Yogurt Swirls 128
Fussy eaters 34

G, H

Golden Crunch 59
Good eating habits 33
Halloumi & Pitta Salad 77
Ham & Egg Cups 64
Ham & Pea Penne 120
Home-made Baked Beans 78
Home-made Beef Burgers 125
Honey 20
Humous & Roasted Red Pepper Filling 81

I, J

Increasing the menu 14
Introducing
  a cup 11
  solids 7
Iron 11, 32

K, L

Keeping pace with baby 24
Leek, Potato & Sweetcorn Purée 48
Lemon Sponge Pudding 139

Lentil Dahl 104

M

Macaroni & Leek Cheese 94
Mango Fool 129
Marlin 20
Meal plans
  From 8 months 22
  From one year old 30
  Toddler 38
Meal times, trouble-free 25
Meat Balls with Tomato Sauce
  124
Meaty Paella 118
Melon Purée44
Merry Berry Cobbler 140
Mexican Rice 100
Milk
  and drinks 16
  matters 9
  needs 16, 25, 29, 37
Mini Banana Pancakes 66
Mini Quiches 88
Miso Noodle Soup 85
Mixed Fruit Compote 133
Mozzarella Tortilla Parcel 90
Muffin Pizzas 87

N

Nutrition needs
  Babies 19
  Toddlers 28
Nuts 20

O

Oat & Vegetable Purée 49
Oat Cookies 135

One year 26
Orchard Fruit Yogurt 54
Organic foods 16

P

Pea & Courgette Purée 47
Pea Soup 84
Peach Crumbles 136
Peach Purée 44
Pesto & Avocado Filling 81
Pesto & Pea Risotto 99
Plaice with Roasted Tomatoes
  107
Pork & Apple Pan-fry 122
Pork with Fruity Couscous 121
Porridge with Apricot Purée 61
Potato Cakes with Beans 67
Potato, Pea & Pesto Pasta 95
Preparing foods 15
Protein
  Babies needs 19
  Toddlers needs 28

Q, R

Quick Banana Ice Cream 55
Quick & Easy Sausage Rolls 93
Quick Summer Pudding 132
Readiness for weaning 7
Real Fruit Lollies 130
Recipes, about 39
Reheating food 15
Rice & Vegetable Fritters 83
Roasted Red Pesto Chicken 114
Roasted Vegetable Tart 103

S

Salmon Fingers with Sweet
  Potato Chips 109
Salmon Frittata 110
Salt 20
Sardines on Toast Fingers 72
Saturated fat 20
Sausage & Potato Roast 119
Seedy Banana Breakfast 60
Seedy Breadsticks 74
Self feeding 21
Sesame Potato Wedges 82
Shark 20
Shellfish 20
Simple Humous 68
Smooth purée 15
Snacks
  Stage 4 24
  From one year 27, 29
Snow Balls 134
Spaghetti with Roasted
  Butternut Squash 96
Spicy Mince with Apricots 123
Squash, Parsnip & Apple Purée
  49
Stage
  one 7
  two 14
  three 18
  four 24
Starting weaning 6
Sticky Date Cake 137
Storing food 15
Strawberry Sundae 131
Strawberry Yogurt Ice 131
Sugar 20, 26
Supplements 12, 32
Sweet Potato Bake 102
Sweet Potato Purée 46

INDEX

Sweets 26
Swordfish 20

T, U

Three-nut Butter 58
Tomato & Bean Dip 70
Tomato & Egg Scramble 63
Tomato & Lentil Soup 86
Tomato & Tuna Gnocchi 105
Trouble-free mealtimes 25
Tuna & Leek Frittata 106
Tuna Tortilla Melt 92
Turkey Fricassée 117
Turkey Patties with Pineapple
    Relish 116
Two years 33

V

Vegetable & Pasta Stew 50
Vegetable Soup with Chicken
    Dumplings 111
Vegetable Fingers 101
Vegetarian babies 18
Very first foods 8,
    Recipes 42-45

W, X, Y, Z

Water 10
Weight issues 36

ACKNOWLEDGEMENTS

The publishers would like to thank:

Photographer: Jules Selmes
Photographer's assisitant: Adam Giles
Food Stylist: Clare Lewis

For use of images and equipment:
BabyBjörn, www.babybjorn.com
Mothercare, www.mothercare.com